WHO ARE YOU, AND WHY?
The Evolution of You

BRIAN PENSO

10-10-10
Publishing

Who are You, and Why?

Copyright © 2019 Brian Penso

ISBN: 978-1-09719-949-5

All rights reserved. No portion of this book may be reproduced mechanically, electronically, or by any other means, including photocopying, without permission of the publisher or author except in the case of brief quotations embodied in critical articles and reviews. It is illegal to copy this book, post it to a website, or distribute it by any other means without permission from the publisher or author.

Limits of Liability and Disclaimer of Warranty
The author and publisher shall not be liable for your misuse of the enclosed material. This book is strictly for informational and educational purposes only.

Warning – Disclaimer
The purpose of this book is to educate and entertain. The author and/or publisher do not guarantee that anyone following these techniques, suggestions, tips, ideas, or strategies will become successful. The author and/or publisher shall have neither liability nor responsibility to anyone with respect to any loss or damage caused, or alleged to be caused, directly or indirectly by the information contained in this book.

Medical Disclaimer
The medical or health information in this book is provided as an information resource only, and is not to be used or relied on for any diagnostic or treatment purposes. This information is not intended to be patient education, does not create any patient-physician relationship, and should not be used as a substitute for professional diagnosis and treatment.

Publisher
10-10-10 Publishing
Markham, ON
Canada

Printed in Canada and the United States of America

DEDICATION

This book is dedicated to anyone looking to find
themselves, their purpose, or their destiny.
May it assist them and those around them to build
a happy and fulfilling life.

TABLE OF CONTENTS

Acknowledgments vii
Foreword ix
Magic xi
1. Painting Outside the Lines 1
2. Disconnect 15
3. Reconnect 27
4. The Power of Choice 41
5. Live Your Life, Not the One Chosen for You 55
6. The Evolution of You 67
7. Memory Lane 77
8. Building a Foundation 85
9. Communication 97
10. Character 113
Testimonials 125
About the Author 127

ACKNOWLEDGMENTS

First and foremost, I want to acknowledge my wonderful parents, **Andy** and **Joanne Penso**, for without their protection and guidance, I would have never made it out of my teens.

My brothers, **Jeff**, **Kevin**, and **Mike Penso**, for helping to keep me on the correct path during my wild and oh so crazy years.

All of my teachers who didn't choke the life out of me when I needed it.

Casey Salge, a great friend, teacher, and mentor, as well as one cog in my mastermind group, for pushing me to share the information I have to offer, with as many people who are willing to step out of their own comfort zone, as we did many years ago.

Also, **Don Stubblefield**, for his heartfelt and sincere comments and recommendation to write and publish this book, to share what he saw as valuable information, to the world, when I met him the first time following a lecture I had done in Houston Texas.

Who are You, and Why?

Finally, to all of the authors who put out the great books I found along the way, and all the books I will find in the near future. They have helped me learn to blaze my own paths and find the roads less traveled. Their selfless sharing of knowledge and wisdom, and their true caring about other people's wellbeing, was an inspiration for me to put pen to paper and write this book.

THANK YOU ALL.

FOREWORD

Brian Penso is a maverick; he broke away from the average a long time ago. A serial entrepreneur, Brian knows what it takes to succeed in business. His achievements as a tournament fisherman suggest that he also enjoys personal success. And given all the years of coaching and mentoring that he has under his belt, there's no doubt he's a leader of the highest order.

In *Who are You, and Why?* Brian talks a lot about the choices you need to be making every moment of the day. As he says in Chapter Four, "It's your life—live the damn thing on your terms." This book shows you how to do just that; how to live the life you deserve rather than the one that has been chosen for you.

Who are You, and Why? is not so much a book as it is an algorithm, a clear set of steps you need to take to break out of your comfort zone, to learn to color outside the lines. Brian may use broad brush strokes, but each one of them cuts to the core of a problem you need to solve before you'll be able to become a true leader.

From disconnecting from the negatives in your life to rebuilding your personal support group, Brian shows you what foot to put forward on the upward path to success. He shows you

Who are You, and Why?

how to build a solid foundation for being the leader you're going to become. He helps you evolve. You'll love what you learn about the Power of You.

I highly recommend this book.

Raymond Aaron
New York Times Bestselling Author

MAGIC

Would you agree that everyone loves magic? The mystery. The illusions. The wow factor (How did they do that?). Magic leaves your mind wondering for days and weeks—maybe years. It's fun in some ways and aggravating in others. Why? It's because we know there's a simple answer to how it works, but we just can't figure it out. Hmmm . . . sounds a little like our lives, doesn't it? You just know there should be a simple strategy, an algorithm, you can follow that will bring you success (however you define it). But somehow the steps you need to follow exist in a fog, and you can't see beyond the end of your arm. Why are things like this? Or more accurately, who are you, and why are you like that? What needs to change?

In the coming pages and chapters, we're going to clear up some of life's mysteries and illusions; and, to some degree, simplify them until you become the magician of your own life, time, and pathway. People around you will be truly amazed at the trick(s) you pull off right before their eyes.

Like in magic, life has its mysteries, techniques, and formulas. Some figure them out; most do not. Well-off people are few and

Who are You, and Why?

far between, and tend to be the magicians in our lives. Why is that? The answer is that they simply had better information (and they've failed more times than everyone else, and definitely more than those who gave up on life too soon).

My goal, in the following pages, is to make you the best at whatever you want to do to become the magician everyone else is in awe of, and to help you discover the mysteries, techniques, and formulas that will bring you the success you've always wanted. Are you ready?

1
Painting Outside the Lines

1

You're young, alive, and full of energy and promise. But society has already begun to stifle you, working to get you to conform. Take today, for instance: you're in school, doing a painting, and your teacher has you working hard to color between the lines. She's not having much luck, though. It's not something that matters to you and, truth be known, your motor skills haven't developed far enough that you can do the assigned task. Furthermore, you really don't care what the drawing looks like. All that really matters to you is that you created something. The finished picture is probably quite awful by your teacher's standards, but when you show it to your mom, dad, and aunts and uncles, the response of "WOW!" is the most commonly used. They also say, "Great Picture!" and, "That's Beautiful!" Your family doesn't have any expectations of you at this point, so all is good. However, as time passes, you find that they take on the same attitude as your teacher: you are scolded more and more for not finishing a picture before moving on to the next, or you are repeatedly told that you need to paint between the lines and to put your name and the date in the upper right hand corner of the page.

The *conditioning* is now in full force, and it will never stop. It has also increased in scope. Everything in school is regimented, and you are expected to conform to an ideal of which you have no understanding. Even your parents have hopped on this bandwagon, setting times at home for schoolwork and *chores*. You're expected to become this perfect little person rather than who you originally started out to be.

In truth, your life, as you know it now, started way back when you were first told you could no longer paint outside the lines. Compliance in all things was the ticket if you wanted a new bike, a fishing pole, or a model boat or plane. The same was true if you were looking for a new dress, new shoes, or a Barbie. *Being good* or doing what was expected of you is how you progressed in life to get what you wanted. It was also necessary if you were to fit in. Compliance was how you built a world that was comfortable. And yes, you're still doing it today. In fact, if you have children, you're doing the same thing to them that was done to you. It's how society curtails our independent actions. It's how we are made to conform to the *ideal*.

I want you to do something for yourself. Look back through all the years you've been on this ride called life. Notice the let downs, the accumulation of daily and yearly things that you really didn't want to do in order to get what you wanted . . . working holidays, weekends, and late nights, chasing a thing you wanted, while someone else was in control of your time and purse strings. To keep that job or position, you had to be compliant—agreed? Your boss most likely provided you with a list of expectations when you first joined your company; it was a statement of conformity you were expected to adhere to in order to keep your job and progress in it. If he or she didn't give you such a list, you're in trouble. Why? There are always expectations. If you don't discover what these are in short order, you can expect to find yourself on the outside, in more ways than one.

Next, I want you to recall some of the times you missed out on: birthdays; your kid's first word, first play, first communion, first baseball game or recital; hunting or fishing trips; a day at the spa or a shopping trip; a cruise with some friends. It's a very long list, so I don't want you to get stuck in these moments. Just notice them and move on. They're long gone, and nothing can be done to change history (except to change the meaning of what happened to you so that you no longer carry your past into the present. More on this later.). As you reflect on what you missed, lots of different emotions will fly past. Notice them and move on. I simply want you to take a few moments to see and understand that you've been living a life someone else has created for you. I also want you to arrive at the conclusion that it's now time to start living your life, rather than continue on with the one that has been chosen for you. At least be willing to consider making the changes I'm going to be suggesting in this book. They're designed to help you begin living a different life—one that's based on you making your own choices instead of conforming to those made by someone else. It's a big step, but if I can do it, so can you.

"But I don't have time," you say. "It's too late to start my life over."

That's bullshit. It's never too late. The only thing that can stop you from embarking on this new journey is death, and if you're intent on sitting around and waiting for that event, there's nothing anyone can do to help you.

Time

It's what we do with time that matters. And trust me when I say you have plenty of extra time. You have 86,400 seconds, or 1,440 minutes, per day—the same as every other person on this planet (including the rich ones). I'm even going to help you sort through your days and make the best use of them. We'll cover more about this in Chapter two.

Thoughts

The key to all of this change I'm talking about is to become aware that your mind is constantly full of thoughts. You have 50 to 70,000 thoughts per day, which is 35 to 50 thoughts per minute. These thoughts change so fast that you don't usually notice them. This explains how good days go bad, and bad days go good. Every time you start a good day, you're latching onto thoughts that support such a day; but if something happens that your subconscious mind deems as being bad or negative in nature, your day can turn on a dime. Similarly, a bad day can turn good when a situation elicits good thoughts.

Would you agree that while some thoughts are not so good, some can be life changing? Well, I'd like you to begin taking a little pause when you come across those earth moving thoughts and ideas. Write them down on paper or, preferably, in a journal. This keeps such thoughts in the present. You can now access, recall, and build on these thoughts at any time. Successful people make it to where they are in life, with lots of little thoughts or ideas that add up to The Big Idea. Most of us mere mortals take a little longer to get there, but it's all good. I would much rather build a foundation of concrete and rock than one made of sand and water. The end result is more predictable that way. The same holds true when building a life. In today's fast paced world, there's an "I want it now mentality." But such instant successes are usually short-lived, and lead to undesirable results. You must be willing to take the proper steps and use the proper techniques to achieve the magic we call success.

Proper Failure

Let's get something straight here. There's a big difference between failure and *proper failure*. Proper failure, you ask? Yes. The only way to learn or prosper is to make mistakes, take notes, and adjust the cause. You can do this because, after a mistake, you have better information with which to adjust the cause. Only those who don't learn from failure truly do fail in the end.

Look, it's not a secret: the world is set up for you to fail—plain and simple. The mind control embedded in TV, radio, and newspaper ads so heavily influences you at a subconscious level that you don't know whether to wind your ass or scratch your watch. It's been planned for you by others for many years.

However, most of the successful people I know have disconnected from all that crap. Dropping time wasters like TV, Facebook, Twitter, and Instagram, to name a few, can be an efficient way to reclaim more of your time. We all have daily issues to deal with, without looking for more of them. Why subject yourself to an endless extra supply? Life's meant to be lived by your own choices, not dictated by others.

Change the Meaning of Your Experiences

Considering most of the people in this country live pay check to pay check, there's no shortage of negativity out there to be spread around. Let's look at your contribution to it. You have a choice every day: you can be positive or negative. If your day starts out poorly and goes south from there, take notice of who or what you were thinking of when things turned bad. Then you must do one of two things: *deal with it,* or *disconnect from the supply house of negativity.*

Dealing with the negativity is done by changing the meaning of what's causing the problem. If you hate your job because of the way your boss treats you, then change the meaning of that dynamic. For example, you might decide that the boss isn't necessarily mistreating you: he or she could be reacting to something that's going on at home, or to pressure from above. This may have nothing to do with you. You're just collateral damage. Why not make it a point to try and be positive around the manager, because you want to help? Why not decide you like your job, and deal with the manager as a separate issue? You could decide that your manager is simply an opportunity for you to practice your problem solving skills. You could even decide to not worry about your boss at all, and that you're going to go forward each day with a blank slate, open to whatever positive things the Universe has to offer you.

However, if the bulk of your negativity comes from your workplace, then LEAVE IT! Disconnect from the source of your problem(s). Nobody is forcing you to stay.

"But . . . But . . . It pays so good and . . . and . . . and . . . "

I say bullshit yet again. You stay because you're comfortable, not because you're hungry. You need to realize that this is how people waste a very large part of their lives. They stay in undesirable places because it's easier and more comfortable. Well, you have to make a choice: do you want to be happy and rich, or comfortable and broke?

"But I'm so good at what I do!"

Okay, let's look at that. There's nothing wrong with being good at something; it's being good at something that doesn't matter, and that's the point. People run red lights and stop signs, and speed like madmen or women to get to a JOB that if something happened to them—in most cases—they would be replaced in a few weeks or days. So, take some time right now to reflect on the last five or ten years of your life . . . Are you in the place you expected to be? Be completely honest. The lies people tell us are nowhere near as detrimental as the lies we tell ourselves.

Who are You, and Why?

Where's the negativity in your life? Is it your dissatisfaction with yourself, or is the negativity caused by a person? And if it's caused by something else entirely, don't stop until you figure out what it is. Found it? Now get rid of it. I don't care how; just get it out of your life. Person, place, or thing—get it gone. Then go back and search some more. Ask lots of questions. For example, use the following words as questions: What? When? Where? How? Why? They're the questions you should be asking: What do I desire? When do I desire it by? Where will this thing be? How am I going to get it? And why is it that I want this thing? Or, more to the point of this exercise: What is negative in my life? When does this negativity appear? Where, exactly, is the cause of the negativity? How does it affect me? Why does it affect me? What can I do to get this negativity out of my life? When will I get rid of the negativity? Where will this take place? How am I going to get rid of the negativity? Why will I do this?

What did this exercise teach you? In all my years of ups and downs, the *greatest* lesson I learned was that I create everything in my world—both good and bad. Whatever it is, I create it.

Do you recall waking up one morning and cracking your toe on the corner of the door, and saying to yourself that this is going to be a shitty day, and it was? Now, think back to another morning, where everything was perfect, and you knew this was going to be a great day, and it was. Well, guess what? You created both days, just as you saw them.

Painting Outside the Lines

Let's look at another scenario. You started out one way and then everything turned south, but then you turned it around in the original direction. That was you again. Most people don't give themselves any credit for what happens to them. They're simply asleep at the wheel. You hear people, daily, telling anyone who will listen, how badly their life sucks and that they're victims, everyone is against them, their boss hates them, their spouse thinks they're a loser, and all of them are keeping them down. That's why they can't make it. The victims of the world hang onto that crap like it's pure gold. It somehow gives them value. They say, "I'm not at fault here." Or, "I really do try hard, but it just never works out." Or, "This always happens to me." If they would only wake up and see that they're the ones who are creating their lives. If they would only realize it's just as easy to assign a good meaning to what has happened or is happening to them, as it is to assign a lousy meaning.

There's a silver lining to all this talk about negativity. And I'm going to tell you that life-changing fact. Are you ready? Are you primed? Are you sitting down? Then here's the great, life-changing information: When it comes to negativity in your life, YOU CREATED IT. That's right; you've proven you can create bad shit. Congratulations are in order! Why? Because the opposite is also true. You have the same ability to create the good stuff, the positives in your life. You just need to change direction, and to make some different choices.

Most people think successful people have it all together. That's not the case. They just deal with their issues, using a

Who are You, and Why?

different elevation of thinking. Where you see a problem, they see opportunity or a way to improve and move upward.

So, how do you elevate your thinking? How can you manage to turn your problems into opportunity? One way is to bring other minds into the mix. Let's say you have a great idea but just can't think of a way to implement it. Consider forming what's called a mastermind group, or joining an already existing group that has similar interests to your own. This can really work for you, but you must be willing to trust and share your idea. I know this seems basic, and maybe even a little old school, but it works. You must get other minds than yours working on your problem(s) and then bouncing their responses off you. This can propel your thinking to new heights that you would otherwise not reach. Napoleon Hill, in his book, *Think and Grow Rich,* was the first person to use the word, *mastermind.* He explained that it was the concept where two minds come together to create a third mind, or master mind, which elevates the thinking of both participants. This is very important, as you can't elevate your own thinking by yourself.

Another way to do this is to find someone who has already done what you wish to do, or who has done something similar. Ask for their opinion, and if they are willing to share, listen. Really listen. This is where you'll have the opportunity to elevate your thinking. Finding such mentors is an important effort to make. A mentor can make all the difference in the world, because they've already made mistakes that you can learn from, thus significantly shortening your own journey.

Painting Outside the Lines

Read the works of other business people (or those in your field), listen to their CDs, and seek them out. Their ideas can also take your thinking to new levels. Not having the money or time while building my businesses, my mentors often came to me through these mediums. There's literally a ton of information out there at the click of a mouse.

And whatever else you do, STOP PAINTING INSIDE THE LINES. Break out of your learned comfort zone, and do something different, something you want to create. And have some fun while you're doing it.

Who are You, and Why?

Notes

2
Disconnect

2

The art of disconnecting can be tricky: what's easy to do is also easy not to do, especially when falling back into routines or bad patterns is your default. Everyone wants *easy*, but I can assure you that *easy* often leads to an undesirable outcome. In fact, I heard something in a lecture one day that hit me like a ton of bricks. The speaker told us, "When you do what everyone else does, you get what everyone else gets!" What an eye opener. If you want to be average (living from pay check to pay check and unable to save a significant emergency fund), just do what the average person does. Conversely, though, if you want to be successful, simply do what successful people do: Put some money away for emergencies; find a source of passive income and stick to it (start a business that can run without you; buy income producing properties; invest in the market, or whatever you can think of that has the potential to produce income while you sleep). What else? Some of the most influential people on the planet have refused to conform or follow people blindly. Instead, they blazed their own paths, took the bullets out front, telling everyone behind them to *"come along; it's going to be fine."* (Note: if stumped by this, study the average person and consider doing the exact opposite of what he or she does. Should you stand to lose nothing by using this method, then act! It's called being a *contrarian*.)

Who are You, and Why?

To become a leader—and that is the goal of this book—extreme changes in daily patterns must occur. You won't like, or may not even agree on, the routes you'll be traveling, but I can assure you they're a must if you want true, positive change in your life.

A short story for you: I had a good friend, when I was young, who took some wrong roads, as I did, and ended up in a really bad place. He was the lucky one who lived; the other guy didn't. And my friend walks around with a bullet still lodged in his body. Talk about a wakeup call! He got a second chance, went on to become successful in his chosen industry, and got married and had a son, who he raised closely so that he could be there and help with his chosen paths.

I know you hear stories like this all the time regarding people who push the envelope way too many times and go bankrupt, or who go just that little bit too far, and end up with their lives flashing before their eyes. I, too, have been in scary circumstances, where I put myself in the middle of a true shit storm and was lucky to walk away. Then there are those unfortunates who make decisions based on the opinions of so-called armchair experts, who create a condition known as brain fog, which messes up their own decision-making process; and next thing they know, they're out of control of their environment, and people die, suffer life-changing injuries, go to jail, or other endless outcomes. Sound familiar? It happens far too often.

These poor souls (and their mentors) are not the people you want to follow. Think about it . . . most people choose to interact

Disconnect

with certain other people daily, who they know they shouldn't be around, but these people are so cool, or they have lots of money, a nice car, and are beautiful (on the outside anyway). They're also mean as a cat backed into a corner, and will even stick an icepick in your back if you cross them, or to advance themselves in some way. Trust me: If you have someone like this in your life, you have to sever all ties as soon as possible. I refer to them as parasites. Harsh you may say, but let's look at this for a moment. What do they truly bring to the table for you? I bet you won't find much. If you do, it's a fallacy at best, or maybe a crutch you believed you needed to fit in. Welcome to your true life.

You need to go through your life with a fine-tooth comb. Compare your decisions and actions, at all levels, to those of people you admire, who are successful at what they do. Wherever you find a difference, write it down. Keep sifting through your life, looking for these differences, until you just can't find anymore. These *differences* are going to become your action plan for success. They are the things you'll need to change to become successful. You'll have to put them in some semblance of order: little changes that you know will lead to bigger changes, changes you can make today, changes that may take longer, and changes that are so big they're frightening.

Everyone has a comfort zone, a place they like to be that keeps discomfort (change) at bay. This comfort zone is the first thing that must go. You need to learn to welcome change as a friend, and as a thing that brings you great opportunities. You can get

Who are You, and Why?

rid of your *comfort habit* by working on some of those smaller changes you discovered in the last exercise. Notice how one change will often lead to another, and another, and so on. By the time you work through these small changes, you should be just about ready for another disconnect.

For example, disconnecting also sometimes means a relocation—maybe not as extreme as mine: In 1987, I packed my bags and left home after living in the country most of my life. I had an old truck, $250 in my pocket, three garbage sacks full of clothes, and all my fishing stuff. When I stopped driving, I was 1,250 miles from home, in the big city of Houston, Texas. Talk about a life change. I saw more cars in one day than in an entire year where I came from. Yes, that was very extreme, but it was well needed to insure my survival at that time in my life. Disconnection of such magnitude is rarely needed, but in my case, it was. I know that had I not followed through with it at that very moment, I wouldn't be writing this book.

Take a look at your own life, and analyze where you are at this point. You must look at it to find areas that need the most attention. Look at how you're making your decisions. Or are you more like a ship adrift without a rudder? You know, not making any headway at all, but rather allowing someone or something else to do that for you. If this is the case, you'll inevitably end up on a reef or someplace else you don't want to be.

I'm sorry to say that the biggest part of the population has been adrift throughout most of their journey in life, and are unwilling to take the measures needed to determine a destination and plot a course for it. And they wonder why they aren't happy and living a fulfilling life! Take another in-depth look at your life right now (Yes, I know it's a pain in the ass.). The thing is, one step alone will save you countless years of struggling, and will help you calculate the best avenue or disconnection at this point in your life. For some of you, a good old *pack up and vanish*, like I did, may be the ticket, but only you can decide that. A new start can be very scary, but in many cases, it can be the greatest move you'll ever make, especially if it's in an area that nobody really understands, where there are a ton of opportunities.

But I want to make sure you understand that even if you pack up and move hundreds of miles away, if you take the old you with you, then you'll need to get ready for another nightmare. A change of environment without a change in you is really nothing more than a waste of time and fuel to get there. It will help a little bit for a short period of time, but it won't take long before you're back in the same mind frame you were in when you left. I've met many people, in the last 30 years, who lived the same life I did, who packed up and moved across the country to straighten themselves out (through reading, then running with a new crowd and, finally, diving into any personal development they could get their hands on). Why were we all successful? The key here is that you must realize and fully understand you're your own worst enemy, and that it must be fixed. This is nothing more than a decision, and then you must take action as well. Most people, when they finally make a decision to do something different,

Who are You, and Why?

become professional students and never really take any action, for fear of falling on one's face. The real learning comes from trial and error. You know, the ass kicking we take along the journey to the desired destination we've chosen.

When I'm talking about disconnection, it's not only people themselves; it's also in reference to what you were taught that also needs to be looked at. Do you know why you believe what you do? Times have changed so much in the last 50 plus years. Teaching people that it's a terrible thing to fail, and with the dumbing down of American students, this mentality of thinking was handed down from the misfits or idiots who took control of our schooling industry, with The Elementary and Secondary Education Act that was signed into law, in 1965. Proof of the damage it has done can be researched on the internet, under *historical SAT SCORES*. This will show test results declining ever since. The powers that be, don't want freethinking people. They're much harder to manipulate at the voting polls, and will tend to turn to handouts instead of education advancements. At this point, it's decision time: stay on the path that was chosen for you, or get off your ass and choose the path that best fits your desires.

Resign from social media, newspapers, talk radio (or radio in general), life-sucking TV shows, commercials trying to sell you crap you don't need, and meds for shit they make up, which are worse for you than your so-called or made-up illness. Cut down on power drinks, soda, candy, and sugar, and start eating better. If this is difficult, **contact me at www.whoareyouandwhy.net.** I can

Disconnect

steer you toward a higher quality of life, by changing nutritional direction.

Next, grab some paper and a pen, and start logging your daily activities. Do this over the next few weeks. Note how sometimes you allow yourself to be conditioned/programmed from outside influences—meeting at a bar, avoiding responsibilities, avoiding a significant other or even your children. Take note of the things you allow to happen daily and weekly that control your life. I also want you to listen carefully to conversations. What are people saying, and how? You'll start to notice patterns of negative, hateful, life-sucking communication all around you. This must come to an end. When you're bombarded daily with this garbage, guess what you end up thinking? As said, "Garbage in = garbage out." Talk about putting the brakes on and killing your dreams and mindset: it's worse than cancer, and grows 10 times as fast.

Allowing these kinds of things to enter your life/space, while trying to get ahead, is the equivalent to trying to win a swim meet with a box of rocks around your neck. Cut that shit loose, or perish as well. Now, I'm not saying everyone around you is doing this, but you must identify those who are harmful, and reduce the amount of time you spend with them. Are you going to get flack and criticism? You bet. The crabs in a bucket scenario is everywhere. When people take notice that you're not the same and are trying to improve yourself, that's when the shit hits the fan. The ones giving the most crap were never real friends anyway—more like parasites, and you're the host. You know the

Who are You, and Why?

ones I'm talking about: those who are always borrowing money, have a car that's always broken down, are late for work, and are always sick; who say it's everyone else's fault or that they're out to get them. The world is full of that, just as mine was.

When you start to notice all the bags of rocks you're carrying, and you carry a pair of scissors to cut the connection, that's when things will begin to clear up a bit. Noticing these heavy burdens is half the battle, something that most never do. Those types of issues are not as obvious as a flat tire on your car but are more detrimental. Maybe nobody has ever pointed this stuff out to you, or maybe you didn't want to see it, but the cat is now out of the bag, and you can't not see it, any more than you can choose to dismiss it and return to your miserable, unfulfilling life. And, yes, that is your choice.

The beauty of all this is that you now have the control at your fingertips. It's just a matter of what you do with it. I know this is only Chapter two, but I wanted to drop this bomb at the beginning of this book. I figured if I could get your full attention at the beginning, you'll have a clearer and more open mind for the rest of the information I'll be providing, and the ROI would increase on the money you spent on this book. I want you to have many WOW moments as you proceed though these pages, and that will only happen if your mindset is changed at the beginning.

Pull up your boots, and put on some gloves. It's time to get down and dirty with issues you need to fix, so get your ass to

Disconnect

work by changing what's needed, because nobody else will do it for you. Self-development is a lifelong journey, full of all kinds of ups and downs, but it's the lessons we learn as we grow that help change our path and the paths of others around us. There's nothing more fulfilling, for most people, than to see the increased value and life improvements in the people we stop and help along our own journey.

Some more of the magic we spoke of earlier is to witness the changes in someone that had lost all hope and had no place to turn. We come across them all the time and usually don't notice them, but now, as we progress, we're changing their lives as well as our own. When you fall on your face, and you will, most people will walk around or over you to get past, since they can't be bothered with someone who can't do anything for them. People like that can't be helped; they've never figured out what we have— so smile, disconnect, and move on down the road. Your new life is waiting for you.

Who are You, and Why?

Notes

3
Reconnect

3

How do you make the changes I'm suggesting? When a tire is flat, it's obvious, and you know how to fix it. However, what I've been talking about is a sneaky, life-sucking vacuum that only you can feel and medicate. The good news is that the more you search for this vacuum, the better you'll become at locating it. You'll also become more aware of it as you travel down your new path. This awareness—on its own—is life changing, but when you add a few more tools to your kit, then you're now getting somewhere exciting.

What am I talking about? When you disconnect, there will be a vacuum—a hole, if you like—where the former people and things had a place in your life. This hole will not stay empty; you will consciously or unconsciously fill it up with new people and things. The trick here is to actively fill the vacuum with what you want to be there, with stuff that will work for you going forward. So, I really want to get into the idea that once you've disconnected, you'll need to reconnect in a certain way.

To begin with, you'll need to find some new contacts so you'll have the help you need to further your goals and life's desires. Now, I want to assure you that I'm not saying you need to stop talking to your remaining friends; you're just going to add some

Who are You, and Why?

new ones. You need to have like-minded thinkers in your tool box, who can assist you in getting to your end goals. Note: these new friends you're cultivating must come into your life on an equal footing. By this, I mean you should be looking to add value to their goals as well as to yours; it's a two-way street. The effect you're after is called a *mastermind*. It was explained earlier.

Masterminds are formed to help high-end thinkers bring to bear their thoughts and years of experience to solve issues, build a better part, streamline a manufacturing plant, increase production capacity, etcetera. Many masterminds are created in a formal session, where members consciously and in a focused manner work on each of the member's problems. However, some of the most successful masterminds work in a completely different way. You see, when you get focused on something for too long or too hard, it's best to back off and look at your situation from another angle. This is precisely what a mastermind group helps you do. Some of the greatest revolutions, business ideas, and life-changing moments have come from two guys or gals on a hunting or fishing trip, vacation, game of golf, or luncheon, when they weren't focused on anything but having fun. You see, at times, when it's clear or at idle, the mind can just create or pull in things you've been looking for, from thin air. How many times have you tried to come up with solutions to a problem—where you look for days and nothing happens—then you toss in the towel, and a few hours or days later, you find the solution? I bet it's more than a handful. And when you have other people doing the same thing, the effect becomes even more powerful.

Reconnect

Allow me to explain. The mind is a wonderful, goal-seeking machine. Ask it to do something, and it will work tirelessly to find you a viable solution—even when you're not focused on the problem you've set before it. The trick is to be very specific in what you ask it to do, AND to get other people to work on the problem as well.

The key to becoming successful is gathering the right people to take with you, such as marketing, sales, advertising, and administrative specialists, who have the skills to remove many of the learning curves, and to speed up the advancement process greatly. Finding these hungry people who are willing to do some work, with just a little pay (while still holding down a job that pays the bills) at first, but who have the vision to see down the road, is what's necessary. Keeping the big picture or end result in focus is the biggest key. Note: you can form a mastermind group with someone who's already successful, but you have to bring something to the table that he or she needs just as much (This is hard to do. You might be better off entering into a mentoring relationship with such a person.).

One of the first places to start is to build into your days, weeks, and months some regular networking meetings around your city and the state. This can be an easy way to meet new and helpful people, whether it's a bridge club, wine club, investment group, mothers' group, swim group, golfing foursome, or networking alliance. There's a long list of opportunities that can be found on the internet, in weekly papers, and on community boards. The Chamber of Commerce in your local city may be a great place

Who are You, and Why?

to start, as they will have information on that area, and contacts who could be helpful to your advancement as well. You'll have to spend a little time, but this is an investment in YOU and the growth of your new business.

When like-minded people gather, the tension is much lower, and people are easier to talk to. They may even drop their guards a little, making it easier to communicate with them. You can share little bits and pieces—just enough to spark interest but not enough to give the farm away—and see if they have any interest in what you're trying to do, and also for you to see if they will fit in with what you're trying to accomplish. You'll need to work on your ability to listen (and I mean really listen) to what people are saying. Ask questions and let them finish what they want to say. Do not finish the sentence for them: this is very rude, and you may have interrupted the most valuable piece of data they were going to give you. Focus on the other person (don't tell them your life story—listen to theirs) as that's when real progress is made.

People love to hear their own voice more than anyone else, and most people don't take the time to really listen to other people. It's a lost art (trust me), and talking over people will put a stop to possibly the most valuable conversation of the evening or even the week; so get really good at listening. Mastering this art of listening opens the doors to meet people with contacts or valuable feedback to help lead you to the answers you're looking for. Conversations leave clues—if you're listening closely and not just waiting for the noise to stop for you to start speaking again. Pay close attention for an opportunity to make your next move.

Reconnect

Successful people around the world have found that a NETWORK is the key to building a solid foundation, and also leads to the increase of overall NET WORTH.

When new people come into our lives, we must look very closely as to what they can bring to the table, and what you can take to theirs as well. The successful business people I've met throughout my life have surrounded themselves with like-minded people. Why? Nobody makes it big without the help of others. The whole idea that I can do it all myself, and don't need any help, is so ludicrous; it's like putting a noose around your own neck and jumping off the chair— sudden death is inevitable. If you look back to the early days of civilization, groups of people settled in nearby areas to survive. One person grew wheat, another corn, and so on. Then they would trade back and forth, because one person couldn't grow everything that was needed to maintain their basic needs. Our world was created with small groups of settlers who understood that we must work together to prosper and flourish in life. This thought process seems to have been lost over the years, which is tragic. You need this kind of thinking if you want to survive the inevitable ups and downs life loves to hand us. I'm not saying specialization is bad. To the contrary: one farmer could grow corn better than anyone else, through years of trial and error, while another could grow wheat like no other. Do you see that the group prospered with each person doing what they did best? That concept is just as important today. When someone needed a barn built, everyone showed up—men, women, and children alike. All people played a part in the construction and completion of the work that needed

Who are You, and Why?

to be done. When harvest time came, the same process was used: people knowing that if the farmer lost his crop, everyone would suffer that loss, not just him, and the entire group's existence and survival could be in jeopardy. *"Teamwork makes the dream work"* is a concept you need to revisit frequently if you want to make it big in the business world. Each person bringing their strong points to the table is like adding rocket fuel to an engine.

The problem of selfishness in people over the last forty years has run rampant, and also has decreased the potential for true success, basically hampering any project from the start-up point. Three out of five start-up businesses fail drastically or go bankrupt in the first few years, mostly from bad or improper research, and lack of marketing skills. I was told once (and nearly forgot it): *You can't solve a problem with the same elevation of thinking that created it.* You need the input and expertise of others. So, your ability to talk to others is key, and if you have a problem with communication, you'll need to overcome it. I'll also let you in on another secret: *Your level of success/income is parallel to your ability to communicate.* Communication either makes or breaks most relationships. You can improve any relationship today, right now, by putting into practice some of these quick tips for improving your communication. (We'll go into this in more depth in another chapter.)

1. Stop and listen to the person who is speaking. Give them your full attention.
2. Force yourself to hear what they're really saying.

3. Be open and honest in all your communications.
4. Pay attention to physical signals, because most communication is nonverbal.
5. Stay focused in the here and now, instead of somewhere in your head.

I really want to make sure you understand that reconnecting is another way of changing your surroundings and increasing the value within your own life. With new people and better information, life has a way of coming together in an uplifting way (better attitude, better focus, and vision is much clearer—all keys to the success you're looking for). Having the end in mind is essential, as without a destination, there's no focus, and that will lead you down many worthless roads, with no real progress. Most people have blinders on and never notice the damage the people next to them are doing.

A Mastermind Group

In a mastermind group, the group sets and owns the agenda, and each person's participation is vital. Members give you feedback, help you brainstorm new possibilities, and set up accountability structures that keep you focused and on track. You'll do the same for them. In this way, you'll build a community of supportive colleagues who'll brainstorm together to move the group to new heights.

Who are You, and Why?

There's the potential for you to gain tremendous insights that can improve your business and personal life. Think of your mastermind group in terms of being an objective board of directors.

A mastermind group can provide:
- benefit from the experience and skills of others
- confirmation that you're making the right decisions and taking the right actions to achieve your goals
- accountability and monitoring of your progress
- a valuable support network
- a sense that there are others like you out there
- you with the means to create a positive attitude

Who should create or seek out a mastermind group?
Those who:
- have a similar interest
- have a similar skill set and/or success level
- are determined to make this year extraordinary
- want to nail or surpass their goals
- are willing and able to accept change
- are eager to commit to the mastermind group members

Note: Mastermind groups can meet in many different ways: in person, through video conference, on the telephone, or via social media. Once-a-month meetings are the norm. Look for motivated people who are willing to help and support, and show up for every session. Before allowing new people into your group, ask the following set of questions, and make sure the vote from the existing group is unanimously in favour of the applicant.

- Do you have a mission or vision statement?
- What goals do you have for the next three years? How committed are you to these goals?
- Do you actually have time to participate in the mastermind?
- Why should our group accept you?

Ask people, who aren't participating up to the group standard, to leave the group, and do it quickly. Such a member can destroy the group dynamic.

You should select a competent facilitator to guide the conversations. You can also charge a fee for being in the group. It will make sure that only serious applicants apply.

And, finally, don't be in a rush to fill the chairs. You want to attract and choose quality people with good experience and valuable information. This may take some time, but remember you aren't in a rush to do this. When you rush, you can make grave mistakes, and you've already had enough setbacks in life and don't want to create even more. I understand you want a speedy recovery, but willy-nilly decisions will just lengthen the journey.

Who are You, and Why?

You must slow down to go fast, as they say—quality trumps all else in this equation. So, get out there, make some new friends, and build your own million-dollar group. They are waiting for you to show up.

Notes

Who are You, and Why?

Notes

4
The Power of Choice

4

This chapter is going to open your eyes to the whirlwind of decisions you make on an hourly, daily, and weekly basis. We all want big incomes, toys, and the feeling of security as we think it should be, but very few are willing to make the commitment and put in the time to do so. Every morning, you have a choice to make: Are you going to do the same thing you did yesterday, or are you going to step out of the daily routine that got you stuck in the first place? This can be a crippling decision, because if you are like most people, you're mostly comfortable and dread the changes you need to tackle. In general, people also tend to justify their pain and unhappiness, saying, "It's always been this way, and I can't do anything to change it." Your complacency is the biggest killer of your dreams, since you've been molded to not push too hard or dream too big—"Ohhh, don't go out on a limb too far, just in case it breaks."

This is the mentality of the poor that's been handed down for generations and has destroyed the will of many powerful minds that agreed and never ever had a chance. I have a few questions for you: ARE YOU TIRED OF BEING COMPLIANT? ARE YOU READY TO TAKE CHARGE? ARE YOU READY TO STOP TRYING TO MAKE EVERYONE ELSE HAPPY BUT YOURSELF?

Who are You, and Why?

Many people work and live lives of acceptance: agreeing to things they don't want to do, refusing to speak their minds on issues, afraid of offending someone or some group, and worrying about what people will think of them. If they aren't paying your bills or paving a dream life for you, who gives a shit what they think; it's your life—live the damn thing on your terms. This all may seem harsh, too bold, arrogant, cocky, or any other word you want to toss in, but it's what it takes if you want your life to be directed by you. The biggest thing you need to understand is that you have a choice in the matter. You can continue to fail, not living the life you want, or you can jump in with both feet and get your ass running toward what you want. This is a daily battle that successful people handle as things come along, knowing that if they refuse to deal with whatever the issue is, the journey will come to an end faster than it got started. Success is for those—who are few and far between—who understand they're holding the reins of this wild stallion we call life, and must keep in control or go on a very wild and bumpy ride, with an unknown destination. You've been making a choice to sit on the sidelines way too long and, therefore, are not living the dream life you want. Aren't you tired of that? Come on, it has been going on far too long, and that was your choice until now.

Aren't you glad you picked up this book? Today is a new day on a new journey. You're now learning you have much more say and control than you ever expected. If you get nothing else from the following chapters, remember that control is pure gold and has more value than you could ever imagine. Seeing this explained this way for the first time, or even looking from a different angle

The Power of Choice

than you have been, should be giving you a feeling of euphoria, happiness, satisfaction, and maybe even goosebumps. You may even—for the first time—find yourself looking through a clearer lens that you've created with new hope. Now, it's been said that hoping just gives you more hoping, without action, but we're talking about having new hope, along with the actions or steps already revealed, and that alone is life changing and will lead you down an entirely new path, to self-satisfaction and a sense of accomplishment that you've been looking for.

Congratulations. I'm going to tell you a short story to see if it fits any scenarios in your lifetime . . . In one of the few jobs I've ever had in my 53 years, I started at the bottom and moved up rapidly to upper management status. I saw many issues that could have been fixed or modified a bit to make us more profitable: daily routines streamlined for better production, better customer care, even better merchandising of the sales floor. Everyone looked at me like I had two heads. "Who do you think you are, son?" they asked. "That's crazy. The people in charge of this division have 20 years of experience, and we don't need your opinions." Now, the guy running the division was in the hip pocket of the kings and queens above, if you get what I'm spreading here (top management). I'm not really sure he had the brain power of a flea, or could pour water out of a boot with the directions on the bottom, but he led with an iron fist and always knew best. At this point, I knew I'd hit a roadblock, and another choice had to be made. The company wouldn't be around very long unless they canned his ass, or he began to listen to the people who truly knew what was going on. I saw the light at the end of the tunnel. It

Who are You, and Why?

wasn't relief. It was a train coming to squash all of us, like bugs on a windshield (It was game over.).

So, I had to make a choice at this time that best suited my survival: stay and perish with the rest, or move on. I fought this battle for about 6 months to a year, at which time I tossed in the towel and focused more on the company I had started to build WHILE WORKING there. I had a game plan and some great ideas, and I started moving on them. I had just walked away from a good paying job and had dived headfirst into my own life path, with no financial support set up. Let me tell you, about a week after I quit, reality had set in, and I said to myself, *"What the hell have you done!"* Scared shitless, I had no other choice but to get my head screwed on straight and get busy.

For the next few years, the path was full of ups and downs, washed out roads, trees blocking the way, liars and cheats, vehicle break downs, lost checks, and stolen products at a trade show. This list could go on for the next few pages, but I think you get what I'm telling you. Was it easy? Hell no, but OMG, it was so worth it. That was the greatest move of my entire life. I didn't know it would happen at the time, but I haven't had a job since.

Before we move any further, did you notice, a few sentences ago, when I said WHILE WORKING at another job? I had made another life choice to start a side business while punching a clock for someone else, creating a backup of income if something ever happened at the place I was working. If that job fell through, I figured I would have enough income to pay the bills until I found another JOB (small thinking). I was still working on getting my sea legs stable in the business world, and I didn't see when I started it that it was the full-blown, monster money-producing venue that it became later on.

This decision led me down other roads to money-making opportunities and investments that would have never come along had I not chosen to take a chance and jump all in. The path also led me to become a life/business coach, public speaker, and products and systems trainer for many different companies, simply because of the learning curves I've overcome throughout my journey in the business world. If you add up what I spent on thousands of hours of personal development, reading, lectures, books on tape, and private mentoring with people, who had what I wanted and who were willing to help me, it was in the hundreds of thousands of dollars. I will tell you I wish it had been twice that, as I would have gone much faster on the business building journey. I would also have listened to the many people pushing me to produce the very book you're reading now, much sooner than I did.

Spilt milk, as they say . . . I should have done this, I would have gotten that, if I had only (you fill in the blanks). Everyone has this in their past, but it's your privilege to make the choice to wash your hands of all the past issues and get focused clearly on today. The power of choice is in every minute, hour, and day of your life. It's what you do with, or not do with, that matters. I personally used my JOB to finance my own business. Folks, the banks wouldn't give me a loan for a fudgsicle at that point in my life. I had dreams and desires so big that I had no clue how

Who are You, and Why?

I would ever get there, except through pure determination, grit, stubbornness, and never accepting my numerous failures.

Another part of my reason for the choices I made that I haven't told you about yet, is that it was my main goal to fish pro bass tournaments against my idols I saw on TV. As a young man, this was the driving force for every one of my decisions. After many years of hardships and struggles, I had made enough money to have my shot at the big leagues of competitive fishing, and I traveled the USA, fishing many of the lakes I saw as a young man. That alone proves that when you stay focused on the end goal, it's obtainable, even for an old country boy with no idea of how to get there.

That journey was full of adventures and new mountains to climb, and challenges I never saw coming, but I met some great people, and made new life-long friends that I still speak with daily. In some cases, I saw parts of the world I would have never seen had I not pushed through all the problems and issues that arose, and continued on my chosen path, with the end in mind. Had I not looked forward in my life, at my goals and such, I would have never taken that leap. Now, you may be asking yourself, CAN I DO WHAT HE DID? Well, we're four chapters into this thing. You'd better have the correct answer. If not, go back to Chapter one and start over. Just kidding of course, as we still have a number of chapters to go.

When I was very young, my father, Andy Penso, would say, "Let's not put the cart in front of the horse." He has lots of

The Power of Choice

sayings like that, which I didn't understand for the longest time, but they make complete sense today. He was simply saying that we shouldn't get in a big hurry or have preconceived ideas on something we have no clue about. A new idea is exactly that: NEW. You have to look at the idea as it is, and then—with time, research, and a little masterminding—you create something from thin air, based on the original thought you had. When you see something on paper or computer, which comes out of your thoughts, it's very enlightening. The art of creation we all have is limitless, if we just get out of our own way. This is the part of Chapter one (coloring outside the lines) I was referring to.

Whether you realize it yet or not, you are amazing—a true BAD ASS—with a super computer sitting on your shoulders. I bet you can think of at least a handful of items that got shot down when you took them to your boss or upper management. Then, a few weeks or months later, the person you told it to had this great idea that he or she ran up the flagpole, and is now the hero, and you never said a word to anyone about it being YOUR idea. That was a CHOICE you made as you were worried about losing your job or upsetting someone. HELLO; it was yours to begin with. It's things like unethical behavior, no morals, lies, and lack of character that we choose to put up with in the workplace that puts us behind the eight ball, which will cause most to bow out of a JOB. The dog-eat-dog environment of the corporate ladder is something I just never understood: how people think it's a good idea climbing a ladder, with no clue what the wall is made of that it's leaning against. Look at all the opportunities you've passed on in the last few years, and ask yourself, "What if I took that chance? Or spoke up at that meeting? Or asked someone I really like out on a date?" There are endless questions I'm sure you can ask yourself at this point in your life. YOU must decide between continuing to sit on your ass and take orders from those who want you squashed, or to belly up to the bar and get moving. The power of choice is now at your feet. What are you going to do with it??????

Perhaps this is the place to talk a little more about the power of choice.

You have a choice you can make, every second of your day. It's a choice that may be answered in three different ways: yes, no, or maybe. The question implied in those answers is: "Will I do this?" It's a question that may be applied across the board, in any situation, and that is a direct response to the thoughts you are having in any given moment. "Am I going to shout at my wife?" Yes, no, or maybe. "Will I say this to my boss?" Yes, no, or maybe. "Will I buy this tie, even though I don't have the money for it?" Yes, no, or maybe. "Can my business withstand this much needed expansion?" Yes, no, or maybe.

I actually refer to the choice of "maybe" as sitting on the fence and making no choice at all. But we all know that *no decision* really is a decision. Why do we know this? Because *no decision* still produces results; there are consequences to whatever you choose to do in the moment, whether it's yes, no, or maybe.

Now, once you realize the power of choice, and that you really can choose your own path in life, something spectacular arises. It's

The Power of Choice

the possibility of defining the meaning of what has happened to you in the past and what is happening to you in the present. That's right; you can choose the meaning of what happens to you in life. In reality, there is no meaning in life that you don't put there. You have the right and the ability to go through your memories and take all the garbage—the hurt, the anger, the hate—and change the meaning of what happened to you into something positive. And when you do this, you actually reach the point where you can leave the past behind, rather than always carrying it forward into the present. Let's look at an example.

I have a friend who knows a woman who was raped. For many years, she carried the hurt and the degradation, and the anger and the hate, into each day. She wore the results of what happened like some kind of cloak. Then she attended a seminar (I won't name the company) that taught her that life has no meaning. The only meaning it has is what we assign to it. This meant that she could change her feelings and actions that were a result of that night so many years before. When she realized this and actually experimented with the idea, she was amazed. She decided that the rape had no power over her, and that it was simply something to log and forget. She could feel joy about her ability to survive, and she could choose to look to the light, every minute, going forward. She started choosing moment to moment thoughts and actions, designed to make living a positive experience. She shed years of anguish while up on the stage, where her instructor taught her to do these things. She cried with happiness. She smiled with joy, and she changed so much that the people who knew her were astonished; so much so, that her family gathered around her

Who are You, and Why?

during the *family* portion of the seminar. It was powerful stuff to watch.

But that wasn't the end of it. This brave woman also learned that she could choose the meaning of whatever happened to her in the present moment. By consciously choosing how she thought, and what she would say or do with such thoughts, the woman became free to consider the unlimited possibilities presented by the future. She became a blank slate, or a clean canvas, on which the future could be written or painted, with no preconceived notions as to what these opportunities were—just the knowledge that she could make them work for her by defining the best possible meaning to what she was experiencing. What a powerful gift!

Notes

Who are You, and Why?

Notes

5
Live Your Life, Not the One Chosen for You

5

Welcome back. You have made it through four chapters already, and you're still here. CONGRATULATIONS.

I hope you're starting to get the picture as to how you've been molded to fit other people's agendas, and it's now time for you to Live Your Life. In the next few minutes, I want you to take the time and write some short/long-term goals and desires. Make them yours, with no outside influences. I want you to do this quickly, as those thoughts that come in first are the ones you need to act on first. Some of these thoughts rushing in have been sitting there a long time and are what you truly desire, but you've been neglecting to recognize or act on them. At this point, all kinds of crazy stuff will come rushing in. Don't think about that part; just write them down. Some will be very extreme, and some not, but they're coming to you first because you have desired them the longest but never confronted them or viewed them as being actually obtainable.

Big or small, write them down—but include nothing based upon what others have told you or said. Remember, you're creating *your* life at this point. Pull all reservations, negativity, and suppression, and anything that has kept you from doing it

Who are You, and Why?

in the first place. I want you to detail everything at this point, getting down to the exact thing you desire. If it's a car or truck, pick the color, engine size, whether it's two or four door—everything to the exact detail. If it's a house, decide how big it will be, in what part of town, in what city. Does it have a pool; is it single- story or three? Or maybe it's a dollar amount you want in a year as income, or maybe starting that company you've had on the back burner all these years. Whatever it is, you want exact details, because the more thoughts you put in, the greater the reality becomes.

Now, most personal development people say to do this, and to pick a time frame or a date. I don't recommend you do that. Lots of times, people pick unrealistic goals for the time frame chosen, and when they don't hit it, they crumble like an old cookie. All goals can be achieved over time, even the unrealistic ones I spoke of earlier. I said that because of time factor, not whether it was doable. Through hard work, education, focus, grit, and the unwillingness to stop, you can put aside all the armchair experts' opinions, and it has never been done before thoughts. Look at some of the greatest people on the planet, who have moved mountains, or finished projects people said couldn't be done. Do you realize everything in your life that you use or see was once a single thought in someone's mind? It started out as a single "What if?" thought, and now it is a reality—the super computer, race cars, sky scrapers, massive ships and boats—all the things that make up your life didn't exist until someone created it. It's now time to use your abilities to create what *you* desire in your life.

Live Your Life, Not the One Chosen for You

Once you've narrowed these ideas down, you'll need details on how you can start going after them. Will you need a specialist, design team, further education, research and design, more money, etcetera? We live in the information age. Anything you need is out there for you to find. It could be in books, social media groups, how-to books, or DVDs, or even in a large library of videos. There are many places that can help you figure your particular thing out. I understand this can all be very scary for you; but trust me, many have done it already, who were in the same boat. They just said, "I don't care what anyone else thinks; I'm pushing forward with my life and ideas." The redirect you're taking is huge. You're stepping out from the beaten path that was chosen for you. Lots of emotions will come into play over the next few weeks and months. You will just have to push through them. What's easy to do is also easy to not do. Staying focused will help with this. Once people find out you're going after what you desire, you'll get flack; and they're going to try knocking you off the rails of success. Anytime you climb the ladder of success, your ass gets exposed and will become a target. Get used to it. Just don't go into agreement; you've been doing that way too long already. When you choose the path you're going to take, you'll have to focus on doing research, reading books, listening to books on tape, etc. But you must remember that knowledge with no action is voodoo. You get much smarter, but you don't get your ideas off the ground.

This is where things get tough. You're going to make mistakes, screw shit up, fall on your face, get made fun of, and maybe be called stupid, but it's all good. Most people on this planet—

Who are You, and Why?

ohhhhh, about 97%—are scared of their own shadow. They're the sheep of the planet and would never step out like you've done. You're the exception; my desire is for you to become comfortable with saying, "I don't care what you think. I'm moving ahead." Even if you fail, you're still better off, as you now have better info for the next crack at it. Long-lasting success doesn't come overnight. It took me 15 years to become an overnight success, and that's the reality of a true, long-lasting, profitable journey that will stand the test of time. It takes as long as it takes. Now, don't get stuck on the 15 years: you're getting guidance that will speed things up. Don't worry about how long it will take. The journey will play out as it should. Things will line up when need be and not a second sooner. Keeping your eye on the prize is the most important thing. Never lose focus. For if you do, I think you know where you'll end up. Do you know that most millionaires lost everything and, in some cases, did so many times before they hit the summit? The only thing different between the rich and the poor is that the rich failed over and over, and just never gave up until they figured it out. That's what successful people do. The poor say that they got lucky or were in the right place at the right time, or their daddy left it to them.

And jealousy or ignorance? That's just someone speaking before actually collecting accurate data before opening their trap. All kinds of garbage will be thrown at you. Just stay focused, and let the negativity roll like water off a duck's ass.

Everyone wants it yesterday, but they just don't realize that success comes at a rate of speed that your mind can handle. I've seen people make piles of money and not have the experience one needs to handle it: blowing money left and right, thinking the spigot won't run dry. When success comes, the mindset must follow in order to make decisions on what to do with the influx of income. Do I buy better equipment, a faster computer, a multiline phone system, a better filing system? That can be a long list, and can be fine-tuned as the money comes in. Now, I'm not saying to spend it like there isn't an end to it. I'm just saying that those items are all important, but prioritizing will be a must, so as to get the most bang for your buck. These kinds of decisions will come through time and experience as you gain more knowledge on your path of success, or maybe through that mentor we spoke of, in a mastermind group. When we look at spending money, time and effort must be put in to make an educated decision as to what increase in production or delivery, or "X", this purchase is going to create for the company.

Consider yourself fortunate that you found this book or someone referred it to you. You could have gone on for years doing the same thing and never realizing you had it all at your fingertips the entire time—it was just that nobody ever told you. Many successful people keep the information I'm sharing with you under wraps or tucked away in a vault. Not me. I think this life-changing information should be shared so those with the guts and willingness to improve themselves have a much greater chance at becoming the person they truly desire to be. A large number of people around the globe have great ideas or dreams but never really see a way to pursue them, or really have no clue where to look for answers or even guidance; and to me, that's a

Who are You, and Why?

shame, and very sad. Just think about someone's amazing idea or life-changing improvement that went undetected, or ended up packed away in a drawer, never to be found.

The main reason I wrote this book is for people to understand just how GREAT they really are, and to show them that the only limitations they have is in their own minds. Now is the time to call BULLSHIT on all the negative, non-productive, and unhelpful criticism that you've been fed your entire life, from many suppressive so-called experts, telling you to not take chances or go after your goals. Most of these people never really produced anything of great value, or changed the world in any way, shape, or form.

I, myself, love proving people wrong when they say something can't be done or there's no way that will work. I just laugh at them and say, "Sit back, and I'll show you how it's done." This alone is entertaining as all get out. The looks on their faces is priceless, but the self-satisfaction is a feeling like no other. The haters are going to hate. We will never fix that, but we can leave them in a pile of dust in the rear view mirror as we speed down our newly created path to freedom.

I just got off a Monday night conference call while on a short break from writing. I love it when people get out of their own way to explore new information and ask questions. This is the starting point for a new life for them. Being a multiple business owner and business coach for many years, I still believe I learn more every time I teach. I see where I need to improve my ability

Live Your Life, Not the One Chosen for You

to deliver and better serve those around me. I LIVE my life daily, always trying to improve my skills with reading, lectures, and speaking with my mentors. It's my way of giving back to the Universe, as I know I will never outgive what I get. This is my way of life—the one that arose from the decision I made many years ago to live MY LIFE—not one chosen for me. It has been a gratifying journey to say the least. There's something comforting about going to bed after a long ass day, satisfied that I gave as much as I could and changed as many lives as possible, but also looking forward to the following day, knowing that even greater challenges will be waiting for me when I rise. Now that you are on your path and creating the new life chosen for yourself, think of how many lives you'll change along the way: hundreds, and maybe even thousands. And that number, my friend, is solely up to you. Your limitations are only in your mind.

We all have them, don't we? Limitations, I mean. These are ideas or beliefs that we've adopted throughout our lives that, in some way, keep us within our comfort zone and out of what appears to be dangerous waters. But are those waters really dangerous? That's the crux of the matter, isn't it? Are you going to be content to wade in warm, safe waters all your life, or will you take on some discomfort to strike out into the cold, deep waters, toward the enticing, far shores? Getting different results, and ignoring so-called limitations, is often difficult—more than you might imagine. But is that any reason not to pursue your dreams of being a different kind of person and creating a different sort of life? I say, "No!"

Who are You, and Why?

The world needs more people like you: people willing to forge out into the unknown, with a firm purpose in mind, and the skills to keep the baying dogs behind them. This book's all about that. It's about helping you to create your own life from this moment onward. And it's about doing this successfully. Each chapter builds on a kernel of truth: an idea that has the power to free you to act. Don't be fooled by the simplicity of some of these truths; each is powerful in its own right and can truly revolutionize your life.

Live Your Life, Not the One Chosen for You

Notes

Who are You, and Why?

Notes

6
The Evolution of You

6

Welcome back. You've proven that you really do want to change your life and are sick of settling. It's going to get really interesting over the next few pages as you begin seeing the path you've taken to this point. Your conditioning started back around the age of two, with discipline forced upon you to fill the needs of parents, aunts, uncles, teachers, etc., but the worst conditioning is that which you placed on yourself.

We hear people say, "I've just always been this way." Maybe you were the fat kid, or you were shy, had four eyes, or wore hand-me-down clothes and didn't fit in with the rich brats that had everything handed to them. Daily badgering takes its toll on you, and you start thinking that it is all true, and go into agreement with it. That's how you get the 30-year-old who gains three pounds and thinks he or she is fat. It's also how you get those who have to have all high-end clothes to make sure they fit in with the cool cats at work or at the gym. This all comes from the past, and was built like an onion (Many layers build up over time, and we just don't see it as an issue.). Trust me; it's a bigger issue now than when it started. You're still hanging onto these things when, at this point in your life, you truly can put them to rest and move on. Easier said than done, you say? Well, you can call bullshit on it, and change, or put this book on the shelf and

Who are You, and Why?

stay unhappy and move onto the next book, where you won't find the answer either. You have the correct book in your hand. The missing link is your mindset and the willingness to take action to fix the issue. That's your choice at this time.

We fail to realize the restrictions that have been created by ourselves and others. The way you make your bed, hang or fold clothes, dress yourself, brush your teeth, or even how you act in a public gathering—everything is done on autopilot, through conditioning. Being a life coach for many years, I ran into this kind of problem daily: "Oh, I can't do that," or "I can't talk to people," or "My parents never allowed me to speak my mind," or "I hate to read; therefore, I can't do this life improvement course." These are crippling conditions that people accept as fact or truth. In some cases, they were forced to do something at an early age (in their best interest) that made them put up the walls in those areas. Let's say you were forced to read at an early age instead of going out and playing with friends. You conditioned yourself, at that point, that reading was bad, so you stay away from it. You carry that as truth when reality is so far off the beaten path that you stay stuck. Reading is the key to learning everything. It gives us the opportunity to collect information from someone who has already been down this path, and that leads to true shortcuts in educating ourselves in a chosen field. A project at work, an invention, a hobby, or a business idea can be accelerated simply by reading, to get ideas or to increase your ability to create the final outcome that speeds you down the path of life.

The Evolution of You

I see people trying to take other less healthy shortcuts, thinking they'll get the end results faster, but usually their efforts are nothing more than a major setback, full of aggravations and, in turn, extending the turnaround time. Everything we do is systematic in some way, shape, or form, based on how we were raised. I personally refused to get things crammed down my throat. It's why I spent so much time in detention or standing in a corner facing the wall (that was SOP for me on a daily basis). Most of the truly successful people I know and have met through the years, walked the same path. We allowed a little conditioning, but we used it to our advantage to get what we wanted. It kept the controllers happy to some degree, and feeling in control at the same time.

Take a few minutes, at this point, and write down some of the daily routines you've placed on yourself, or that someone has placed on you through past conditioning. This is key to raising your awareness level. And once we see the routines, and identify whether or not they are helpful or unhealthy, we can start to fix them. Look for things that you tend to do automatically, without thought. If you're a student, it might be your study habits. If you're a businessman, it could be the way you greet salespeople or treat your subordinates. If you're an entrepreneur, it could be the way you project your brand. It could also be something much simpler, like what you eat for breakfast or whether or not you take coffee breaks throughout the day. Anything that affects the outcome of your day, which you do on an automatic basis, is fair game. Or, perhaps, it's something that you do that really makes

Who are You, and Why?

you uncomfortable, that you already know works against you. Write it down.

Well, I trust you did the exercise. If not, please do it. This is key to locating issues at hand that need your immediate attention. And once aware of them, you can begin taking action. This is going to take some time, so pick one that irritates the hell out of you, and stay focused on it, practicing daily reversing of whatever it is you don't like. You'll stumble at first. Just remember that you or someone else created this a long time ago. There will be lots of programming to be reversed. The longer you stick with it, the better the results, and once you feel you have a bit of a handle on the first one, pick the next issue on the list, and so on. You have the fastest, most powerful computer in the world resting on your shoulders. You just haven't been using it to your advantage. As aggravating as it is, THIS MUST BE DONE if you really want change in your life. You can't move into a shiny new future with the old tarnished you. Realizing it's going to take some elbow grease and time is most important; you didn't get this way over night, and you won't be fixed overnight.

Another way to consider the problem is that you don't change routines, habits, or beliefs, in a vacuum. When you stop one behavior, you must always replace it with another behavior, preferably one that counters the routine, habit, or belief you're trying to eliminate. You can tell whether the automatic behavior is a routine (It's a set of behaviors that gets a certain thing done in a defined way.), a habit (It's usually a specific behavior that you repeat consistently and automatically, which is tied to some specific result,), or a belief (It's an entire array of behaviors that are triggered by some specific idea, such as, "I'm stubborn," or "I don't like over-friendly people."). People often say you must practice the new behavior for 30, 60, or 90 days, until it will also become automatic. But the truth is that it takes as long as it takes. If the routine or habit or belief was laid down in childhood, and you're now middle aged, the behaviors involved aren't going to just disappear. You're going to have to counter them, on purpose, every time you automatically start the routine or find yourself bowing to the habit, or when the belief is triggered. Yes, it's hard work, but it's so worth it in the end.

Note: there are also automatic behaviors known as rituals. You'll know you've discovered a ritual if it meets the following definition: A ritual is an act or series of acts regularly repeated in a set precise manner. Someone who has OCD, or is someone you've heard referred to as fastidious, has a lot of rituals. Baseball players are famous for them. Carpenters tend to do certain things in exactly the same way every time, in order to avoid making mistakes. These, too, are rituals. I mention rituals because they are notoriously hard to change. Just know that if you have a ritual you've decided is holding you back, patient alteration of the set of behaviors, every time the ritual is triggered, will result in its removal. It just takes time and a little effort.

I feel, at this point, you are getting more control over the reality you're now in. You may even be able to see the direction in which you want to go, and are actually getting the tools necessary to do so. My life-turning event came along in the early

Who are You, and Why?

80s, after someone shared similar information that started my transformation journey. Learning that I was my biggest problem was the most enlightening experience of my life, and has enabled me to build multiple companies, with more on the way. It has also allowed me to help others do the same. I've been self-employed for over 30 years now, and I love the freedom I've gained (financial freedom as well). No alarm clock is a very nice way to live, and yet I still get things done by prioritizing the most important things. This will come to you as well, after a little reconditioning on your part. Well, we've reached the end of yet another chapter, with more progress on the way. I recommend you take a day off at this point to regroup and reflect a bit more on your life.

The Evolution of You

Notes

Who are You, and Why?

Notes

7
Memory Lane

7

Well, hello again. I'm happy to see you're pushing through. This chapter may be the shortest or could be the longest one yet. That will depend on how focused you are. It will, for sure, be the most emotional. So, please, make sure to do the upcoming exercise, as it will aid in getting you back on track and focused. There are not many paragraphs in this one. I'm going to take a little break from writing and put you to work (since it's all about you and your goals).

It's a fact that our lives are made up of our daily thoughts, and it's true that what we think and focus on MOST is the determining factor of the outcome. If your thoughts are negative, then your day will be full of negativity. But positive thoughts of future success, ideas, a vacation, or a bad ass car will keep you focused even when the day doesn't go just right. Your goals, focus, attitude, and willingness to push on is the do all and be all creator of the results. Nothing else matters. I see it daily, where people have given up on lifelong dreams after being beat down and discouraged along their journey. It has been very upsetting for me to see talent go to waste that could have changed the world. At this point, I think you've had enough settling in your life, and you should be willing to make the changes necessary to pick up your dreams again.

Who are You, and Why?

It's so satisfying to see people such as yourself wake from a life of sleep walking, realizing you've had most of what you needed, to accomplish anything you really wanted, but never had anyone take the time to point it out until now. You're welcome, and I really do wish I had produced this book back when I was asked to write it many years ago, but that's water under the bridge and is one thing I can't do anything about but apologize for the delay. The good thing is that I did wake up and listen to those around me who knew that what I had to offer was life changing—even though I didn't see or believe it myself. Thank you all for pushing me enough that I finally woke up to the possibility. It was pointed out to me that you can never give more than you get, so I asked myself, "How can I give more out in value, and reach even more people, at a much faster pace?" The answer came after many phone calls to my mentors; all agreed it would be in a printed book. I didn't have a clue how to do so, but I'm going to tell you a short story about how this came to fruition.

I had made the decision and really just put that thought on a back burner, still unsure if I had made a commitment to something I wouldn't be able to do. I was on the computer one day, on a social media page, when I saw an advertisement for a personal development group that was coming through my town and was offering high-end discounted tickets. I purchased one, put a reminder on my phone, and never thought any more about it. Well, my notice went off a few days before, and I was excited and ready to go and see what else I could add to my tool box of self-development tricks. Nowhere in the ad did it have anything about how to write, print, and publish a book. Talk about law of creation at its finest! All I did was make a decision to write the book, and what did I pull in? An ad that led me to a 3-day seminar that was personal development based, about how to step up your game and how to share it with the world in a printed book. That's the power we all have and use daily, never seeing its true value and that we can use it to create our own lives. The entire reason for this chapter is to get you to open your eyes and see what you can now create, and to get you focused on what YOU truly desire, not what someone dictates to you. Trust me; the goals, desires, and dreams are still there waiting for you to bring them into your present life.

The Law of Creation (or Law of Attraction as it is more commonly known) is a life-changing reality you want to understand. Basically, the idea is that you take the time to put yourself out in the Universe in a specific way. When you do this, the Universe will do the same thing; it will reach out to you. People who put themselves out in the Universe, by creating ideas, giving their minds instruction, or creating actioned goals, run into more opportunities and coincidences than other people do. This phenomenon is so widely recognized that it is called the Law of Attraction. You heard my story, and I'm sure you can find many other examples, maybe even in your own life.

I mentioned giving your mind instruction. It is your greatest asset. If you ask or tell your mind to do something for you, it will work around the clock to make that thing happen. The better, more pointed your questions or commands, the better the job

Who are You, and Why?

it will do for you. That's why specific goals are so powerful. The Universe will also lend a hand.

At this point, I want you to stop reading and find some old pictures and goals from days gone past that are uplifting, and get your mind running on positive thoughts today. We're going to use these daily from now on. Vacations, cars, boats, a dream house, and maybe that company you've been wanting to start, or an idea to improve an existing company—we're going to focus on some past dreams that got buried along the way, and create a dream board using some of those pictures, and some new ones, from an advertisement, magazine, or even a download from the internet to keep you in the moments. You're going to post this board up in your house so you'll see it every day and be reminded to stay positive. The thing about these magical thoughts is that they're still there. They just got covered up with all of life's wonderful letdowns, the ass kickings we took along the way, and all the negative people in our past. Take as long as you want on this exercise; there is no rush to get to the end chapter. I want you to relive those moments and start dreaming as you did then. You need to dig deep and capture every detail, even with finite points: "What color is the car or boat? How long will your trip last? Who are you going with? Is there water involved; what color is it? What sound is it making? If you're flying to a remote destination, where is that? Is it an island or a beach? Can you smell the water, area, or mountains? Can you feel moisture on your face, or just a mild wind? Is there snow on the mountains, or are they full plush green to the top? Are they rocky or full of trees?" I want you to live these moments as if they have already

Memory Lane

happened and you're standing there at this very moment, because in reality, you've already created them in your mind/life. You just didn't follow through to fruition because of . . . (Well, pick a reason. You have plenty to choose from). You've allowed outside influences to put stops on your life and dreams for many years, and that ends TODAY. If this part takes you a day or a week, it doesn't matter. Don't pass this point until you're done. Many of you will say, "Ahhh, that's a bunch of shit," and move on—BIG MISTAKE. Let me remind you that you've put yourself in the place you are, based upon your thinking. If that's not where you want to be, maybe it's time to drop the *ego and attitude,* and create a new viewpoint. But you do what makes you happy or unhappy; it's your call.

All done? Good. After finding all those flushed or forgotten goals and dreams, we're now going to pursue what you can do to make them a reality. Will that be to get a better job, improve your communication skills, actually get to work on time, work on your character and ethics, become a better leader, or work a little harder and longer to finish your work or project ahead of schedule instead of late or last minute. If you're employed and could be your boss for a day, would you be happy with your work, or would you fire your ass and find someone else to get the job done better and on time? We'll be focusing more on that in the next few chapters, but for now, I hope you enjoyed the journey back through time. It will be enlightening for you to see the many things you've covered up or simply gave up on. See you soon, in Chapter 8.

Who are You, and Why?

Notes

8
Building a Foundation

8

When an architect designs a building, he or she always starts with a solid foundation. If not, it won't be standing long, or it will have catastrophic flaws that will show up later on. The longevity comes from the details at the very start of construction, and has to be maintained throughout the entire project. I'm sorry to say that people in general pay very little attention to their own life foundation, because this lesson and wisdom is very rarely spoken of in today's world. Lots of semi-successful people don't speak of this, mostly out of fear of loss and insecurities about themselves. This is foolish and needs to be dealt with, or they will never create a long-lasting business or happy life. Schooling systems don't teach it either. They are paid to produce robots that are to be released into the work place, not to produce free-thinking people. I am sorry to let you in on a little secret: the world is set up for you to fail and to keep you broke, but I'm betting you figured that out already, and that's why you're reading this book. Let's look at it this way: Check out some of the old schoolers in your industry, who have been around 25 to 35 years. Are they happy? Are they financially independent, travelling the world whenever they want, and truly happy and at peace with themselves? Chances are, they're still slaves to a job they can't stand, but if you would have asked them 25 years ago, they would have thought they'd be running the entire place and

Who are You, and Why?

have a cheese job, making plenty of money each year. Pipedreams, my friend. Many people were sold that poison pill. They were promised the big promotions if they worked really hard and put in the time, but they were then knocked out of the position from an upper management family member, or a snake in the grass they didn't see coming. Like the carrot on the stick in front of the donkey, he never gets to taste that sweet beauty but keeps chasing it, thinking that someday he'll get it. The world is full of broke people who dedicated their entire life to a similar cause and then regretted not taking more chances, when they had many opportunities but instead turned their nose up at many deals. It's a true shame more people don't wake up sooner.

This entire chapter is going to be about you building your foundation to propel yourself, while at the same time working for the man just a bit longer. You're now the architect and builder of the foundation that best fits you, and this will assist in creating an exit plan to a life of freedom, living with intention, and even achieving the fulfilling lifestyle so few ever get to have.

So, we need not cut any corners on this exercise, as finding the problems up front will trim the time drastically. Get some paper and a pen. I want you to make two lists: The first is going to be all your pluses, and the second will be what needs to be improved the most. These lists will be the blueprints for the construction of your next chapter in life. Do this with NO attention placed on any one item. Write it down and move on. This is no time for self-doubt or self-criticism. That's what got you stuck to begin with. This list is your handbook to keep track of all the good things and

Building a Foundation

the bad, and it will guide you as to what direction you need to move in next. This may seem unnecessary to you, but if you can't see what needs to be improved upon, what are the chances you will change anything? None. And then you'll return to your same old routine. So, stop and write up your list now, and then return to reading.

Okay, you should have your list done. Let's look at all the strong points and see what we can do to improve one—even if it's just a little bit. Is there a book, a lecture, or maybe a book on tape, by an accredited author with a strong track record on that subject? Yes, I know you may have to put out a few coins (There are also lots of FREE books and audio books available from your public library—why not take advantage, since your tax dollars are paying for them already.) for it, but successful people know that good information isn't free and is always worth the money—even if you only get one good idea from it.

Go down the list and do the above step on each item. You can review the information out there that appeals to you. Ask someone you know who has some experience, or maybe contact an expert on that item, who can steer you in the correct direction. I'm sure you'll end up with a lot of information to help you build your foundation.

But that's only half of the job. I also want you to start on the second list (things that really need to be improved). Start with the one you regret or hate the most. With that one knocked out, you crack the biggest nut in the pile, which I'm sure will boost you

Who are You, and Why?

the furthest because it's an issue you should have confronted ages ago. With that hurdle out of the way, the rest will be a cakewalk. Of course, it will take time to tackle each and every thing on both lists, and as you do this, there will be new challenges and unforeseen road blocks that will come along. They may as well be added to the lists and handled in the same fashion. One of the greatest lifelong secrets, which the powers above left out and didn't want you to know, is that learning and self-improvement is a daily and life-long journey that only ends when you take your last breath.

I do personal development every single day, and have been for the past 30 years, yet I've only scratched the surface of what I need to learn. Some choose to stop and figure they know it all. Such people actually die at that point but don't get buried till many years later, after a lifelong struggle and unhappy journey.

Let's move on. In the last chapter, you were asked to pull up an idea or dream. I want to focus on that. And we're going to start backtracking a bit here. I want you to ask yourself what you can do differently, starting today, that you haven't done, neglected, or even refused to do in the past. This is a milestone for people who will take the time to really look and see. It should be a WOW moment, one where you recognize that you have been your problem the entire time, and can now fix this. I don't care if you are 17 or 77. This is a life-changing cognition that you can build an empire on top of: a foundation of solid structure you have control over. Good information is the key to all successful adventures, and a must-have going forward. After all, the most

Building a Foundation

expensive information you'll ever get is free from those who think they know. You must take the responsibility for your own future. No more blaming others for your circumstances. If you can't find a solution, then create one.

Let's look at an example of how we can attack one of your ideas. If it's a business idea, we need to gather more info on its basic structure. Does the company or product exist? Or are you going to take an existing idea and make it better? Is it something new that will need R and D? If so, let's look at who can assist you in gathering said information. I'm not saying to push it off on someone else, but who do you know that's great at looking things up or surfing the internet for clues and helpful hints. Don't be in a rush to get finished. The path will be full of clues and ideas for you to work with, even when you are not looking for them. Most of the successful people I've met in my life have capitalized on many small ideas that led to the big one. Do you need graphics done? Let's find someone who's really slick and makes it look easy. You know the ones. They're out there and can do it in their sleep, but you must find them. Maybe it's a friend or someone you met years ago at a party. What I want you to understand is that success leaves clues, but you must always be looking for them. They're not obvious all the time, and many are so small that you can overlook them easily when not focused. Also, never dismiss an idea until you've fully researched it, and even then, don't discard it but file it away. It may be valuable down the road.

The example I just spoke of is one of thousands out there. You must find your own path, paying close attention to everything that

Who are You, and Why?

comes along the way, as you just never know when it will become one of the main stepping stones on your path. I also hope you're starting to see that you have much more influence than you ever thought possible, and that the people you're attracting to the table also have an opportunity to excel. This happens because, in your adventure, true success is based on a group effort, with everyone on the same page. Don't use people like puppets. Cast a vision for yourself and for them. And try to remember that encouragement, uplifting gratitude, and compliments will do amazing things for someone who rarely gets any. With this kind of thinking and battle plan, anything can become a reality. This is how many million-dollar companies have been formed—with just a single idea or a passing thought from a group of like-minded people, working together on a common problem. The poor tend to think success is a matter of luck, and they never see that the fact of the matter is that it is hard work, research, reading, long hours burning the midnight oil, the willingness to push through all the let downs and bumps in the road, and the capacity to work with others to your mutual benefit.

Les Brown, one of the world's top public speakers, defined it best with a poem he wrote many years ago. I think it merits repeating here . . .

> "If you want a thing bad enough to go out and fight for it,
> to work day and night for it,
> to give up your time, your peace and your sleep for it . . .
> if all that you dream and scheme is about it,
> and life seems useless and worthless without it . . .

> if you gladly sweat for it and fret for it and plan for it
> and lose all your terror of the opposition for it . . .
> if you simply go after that thing you want
> with all of your capacity, strength and sagacity,
> faith, hope and confidence and stern pertinacity . . .
> if neither cold, poverty, famine, nor gout,
> sickness nor pain, of body and brain,
> can keep you away from the thing that you want . . .
> if dogged and grim you beseech and beset it,
> with the help of God, you will get it!"

It only took me 15 years to become an overnight success. And the reality is that less than 3% of the population ever accomplish the goals they pursue, simply because they tossed in the towel way too soon. The truth of the matter is that you can accomplish virtually anything if you stick to it; the only thing that can stop you from achieving your goals is death itself. Just think about this for a few minutes: If you turn the power of your mind onto a singular goal, making it the be all and end all of your working life, it's almost impossible to fail. Add in a mastermind group, and I truly believe your goal(s) will become a surety.

Here's another idea . . . Always keep a small notepad near you, so that when an idea hits, you can write it down as soon as possible. Don't wait until later. You may lose valuable details that could have been a game changer, and the thought may not come back around for months, costing you valuable time. At first, keep what you're doing to yourself and the handful of associates you're working with. An idea in its infancy is a fragile thing; and

Who are You, and Why?

trust me when I say there will be plenty of people who will let you know it's crazy and will never work. It's the crabs in a bucket syndrome, hard at work. You know the ones: the haters who never get anyplace, and sure as hell don't want you to get there either. It's sad to think there are people close to you with that kind of shit thinking; but trust me, there are more of them than there are of us, so keep an eye peeled daily. They are nothing but trouble. They'll smile in your face but will stick a spike in your back the first chance they get.

I must commend you on a job well done. You've survived eight chapters, and I trust those have been life changing for you. But we're not done just yet—you have two more to go.

Notes

Who are You, and Why?

Notes

9
Communication

9

What entails the art of communication, and why do so few pay close attention to it? **Communication**: defined in many dictionaries as the imparting, conveying, passing on, and exchange of information, news, instruction, photographs, etc. It's an endless activity, the transferring of some sort of idea or thought between two or more people or groups of people. Different types of communication also exist: verbal, nonverbal, written, interpersonal, and symbols; and many years ago, before any words had been created, hieroglyphics.

Our world, as we know it, all started with the evolution of communication that began with some sort of grunts, hand signals, and drawings in the dirt. Although crude at best, these things worked and were the beginning of things to come. They were and still are the foundation of our never-ending struggles to succeed and survive. Let's think about this: we started many thousands of years ago, in small groups, with the will to strive and push on, learning and growing as a united village or settlement, cut off from the rest of the world. Language developed, but most had no idea of the populations that existed just a few miles away. Communication was limited to the small groups but was enough to get things done within the circle of influencers, and that helped everyone survive, unaware of life beyond the trees

Who are You, and Why?

around them. Then, as people progressed and expanded their territories, other villages and groups of people were discovered. They had food, weapons, coffee, tobacco, grains, and many other items to be traded between themselves, which did not exist for them before the communication line was established. Life became a little easier, and a few luxury items (a new piece of clothing, or shoes, or maybe just a cup of coffee) that we take for granted today made that rough life tolerable at best. With the new long-distance discoveries, extended forms of communication were needed, and the use of smoke signals, loud beats of drums, and two sticks clashed together had an agreed upon meaning, to stay in touch. Of course, runners/messengers soon followed. These were some of the first long distance forms of communication.

As the world expanded even more, greater distance communication was required, and in the 1830s and 40s, the telegraph began to develop. An idea to create long distance transmissions of information, with a series of dots and dashes (Morse code), each assigned to letters, was created; and in 1844, the first message was sent from Washington, D.C., to Baltimore, Maryland. The limitation of wires needed to transmit everywhere led to more creations to transfer information.

Let's move down the road a few more years, to the creation of the Pony Express, on April 3, 1860. There was a weight limit for riders (100 to 125 lbs.), for more speed and less wear and tear on the horses, allowing greater distance traveling in less time. The average time, from pickup to drop off, was 10 days, which was

Communication

much faster than stage coaches or ships in those days. The life span of the Pony Express was only 19 months, but it had an impressive delivery record of transporting 35,000 plus pieces of mail, until its demise, on October 24, 1861, when the transcontinental telegraph line was completed. Fast forward to 1876, with the invention of the telephone opening up even more opportunity, which sparked the beginning of the ever-growing need for even faster, and overseas, communication. The evolution of faster and more efficient means had to be developed, and eventually turned to fiber-optics and cellular systems (almost making the once valuable wires and poles system obsolete), with massive nanosecond speeds, moving billions of wireless transmissions every minute and hour that passes.

You should be getting the idea at this time that communication is and always will be the foundation of all successful actions. However, too much of anything is not good as well. The smart phones of today have retarded verbal communication and have made people lazy. Everyone wants communication NOW. They don't have time for personal communication bullshit. I see people in a coffee shop, sitting at the same table, texting each other and not speaking a single word. The true art has been lost and removed from society, and this seems to be acceptable to the masses. The majority don't want to learn to speak or read books anymore. "Oh, I can find that on the internet!" is a very common phrase of today. The vast majority of our population cannot communicate unless it's on a cell phone, and this is the prime reason for the decline in our society and the lack of responsibility for one's own wellbeing.

Who are You, and Why?

Now, I do agree that smart phones and computers are sources of communication that can be valuable at times, but they will never replace the true value of personal interaction communications. Seeing the person you are speaking with, looking into his or her eyes, and reading their body language (another type of communication), more often than not, can translate a better feel or what's going on than what you are reading or hearing.

Why are some people so much better in sales than others? They've mastered the art of communication on many different levels that others just don't see. Why is it that many quickly promoted people, at any given job, do as well as they do? The most correct answer is their ability to use communication to duplicate what is needed or wanted from management and the clients they are serving. Now, don't get me wrong here. We have all seen the smoke-blowing, lying, cheating pricks who do move up the ranks faster with their sly, charismatic line of bullshit. But they're usually quickly found out and let go, because they just can't deliver what they said they could.

The true communicators of the world use their ears more than bumping their gums. When you're constantly speaking over people, you never really hear what you need to hear; you end up missing the valuable data you need to properly answer the question or request that has been asked of you. One of my mentors told me a long time ago: "You have two ears and one mouth; use them in proportion." That's one of the most valuable pieces of information you'll ever hear if you're in sales and want

Communication

to make a pile of money, or you simply want to learn to survive at another level. Listening is by far the most valuable part of communication; you can take notes on the key issues or facts that the person is divulging, so you can make an educated decision as to what is the best way to assist them in their needs and wants. When you truly listen to every word, it's all in there—the person's concerns, reservations, distrust, anger, joy—if you take the time to decipher it correctly and accurately.

As I had mentioned earlier, we all know someone who can sell matches to the gate keeper of hell, or ice to an Eskimo. This advanced ability comes from mastering the art of listening. Well, I have to admit I wasn't one of them. I was one of those people who talked over everyone and tried to make them wrong. Until, that is, I took a course on proper communication, which opened my eyes to a new life. As I moved on, learning more and more, it began to open doors that once were closed, locked, and nailed shut. Now, my new skills were giving me the opportunity to learn more about what my clients really wanted from me. In my chosen business field at that time, the information I was collecting had a much higher value because I was asking the correct questions, listening carefully to the answers, and taking good notes. I had been overthinking the entire process by assuming I knew what my customers needed, instead of letting them tell me what was desired. My life, at this point, became more focused; and having better, more accurate information sent me on a rocket ride with the expansion of new clients and higher sales, which increased my overall footprint tenfold.

Who are You, and Why?

With the expansion of my business came new challenges and hurdles I didn't see coming. Being a young, uneducated business man, guess what came next? A demand for an even higher level of communication with those who had traveled the same bumpy road I was on, and who were willing to help me. Now, don't get me wrong here; I've heard many different viewpoints, and some of them didn't fit what I was trying to do, but I still took the time to listen, pay attention, and weed out the good from the not so good advice. I'm baffled daily, by observing people beating their heads upon a rock, trying to figure something out to no avail. And they continue on that path for weeks, months, and even years, and never seek advice from those who have already done it. It's been said for years that readers are leaders, and by far the most successful people on the planet, simply because they figured out *"why reinvent the wheel when someone else has already done it before,"* and they can use their hard work to their own advantage. Had I not reached out to these successful people and taken the time to listen closely, I most certainty would have perished like many others before me who were unwilling to learn the ropes.

I now have a question for you: "Are you one of those people who only speak and not listen?" If so, you must take a hard look at this chapter. You can fix your problem with a little bit of applied effort and practice, and some research through communication courses and books. And if you over speak, cut people off, always need the last word, or finish other's sentences, you need to fix these things now! I have found that when people do that, they're insecure in their own life. They are always trying to impress

Communication

someone with a tidbit of information they think is far superior to theirs, knowing they really have NOTHING of value to bring to the conversation; but they grab straws anyway, hoping they have made a good impression. When I'm on the receiving side of that, I do get an impression alright: they're full of shit and really have nothing of value to add to the conversation—so I end it rapidly. I don't have time, and neither do you, for worthless, opinionated, unproved, babbling information from some egotistical armchair expert that still lives with his or her parents at 35 or 40 years old. These are people who have accomplished nothing but think what they have to say needs to be heard by anyone who'll sit long enough to listen.

When you start raising your communication awareness levels, it's not just the listening part that's key. You'll also start to develop a bullshit meter and, trust me, it will start going off more often than in the past. When you really listen to someone, you get dialed into the conversation and will start to pick up little differences, lies, or simply something said that contradicts what they said a few minutes back. Trust me; many just speak with absolutely no thought as to what they're saying, and can't remember what they told you three minutes before. Have you ever had a conversation with someone who took over 15 minutes going on and on, and at the end, you realize they'd been speaking that long and really didn't say anything? Oh yes, there are many of those you'll start picking up on—realizing someone was speaking, and really, all you got out of it was that they were checking to see if their vocal cords were still working.

Who are You, and Why?

The part I want you to see in all this is to be careful to whom you listen. Why? Many bad decisions in our lives come from conversations just like the ones I've been talking about. They can cost us many years of our lives. I'm going to give you another example of what I'm talking about, and many may relate to this. Definitely ask yourself how many times you think this conversation goes on in a day across this country.

> Father: "Son, its time you make a decision on what you want to do with your life."
>
> Son: "Well, Dad, I think I'm going to take a little more time to think about what I want to do. I have an idea but just haven't decided yet."
>
> Father: "Well, you know I've been saving for you to go to college to become a doctor, and that's what you should be thinking about."
>
> Son: "Dad, that's not for me. I hate to see blood or someone in pain, and it wouldn't be a good choice for me."
>
> Father: "I've been busting my ass for years and have sacrificed to make all this money for you to go to college, and I have taken the time to line it all up already."
>
> Son: "I really wanted to go to school to be _____. I would get to travel, meet new people, and help others not so fortunate, and truly make a difference in this world. I've been studying it for years, and I would be great at it."

Communication

> Father: "Have you lost your frick'n mind? You can't make any money doing that, and I'm not going to support you in any adventure other than becoming a doctor."
>
> Son: "Well, I guess that's what I should do then, since you are the one footing the bills. I will just have to get used to seeing all those sick people, and learn to deal with it."

Meanwhile, four years down the road, the kid's in a school he hates, flunking out of his classes because he's not chasing his own dreams and is completely miserable being there. He has flushed four years of his life, and many of his father's dollars, down the swirly tub we call a toilet. Meanwhile, back home, his father is livid from looking at all this money going down the drain, and at a son who's not getting an education. Talk about a waste for everyone. This is the end result of a conversation where both were at fault for not listening and for not saying what needed to be said.

This scenario has repeated itself over and over for the last 100 years or more, and has led to many heartaches, much wasted money, and countless unhappy lives. When we sacrifice what we really need or want to say, for something that someone else wants to hear, it's another form of terrible communication and can cost you many years of your life. It's also the reason for hundreds of thousands of unhappy people in their jobs, family life, and marriages across this country—all because of communication breakdowns.

Who are You, and Why?

We've all heard the stories of the brothers or sisters who haven't spoken for 5, 10, or even 30 years, all because of what someone said or didn't say when they should have. I believe that's crazy thinking and a true waste of life for both, and for everyone else involved. I believe that missing communication can be worse than bad communication, and it can leave someone stuck on something for many years because they don't have the correct information to solve or fix the problem. Therefore, they carry that shit like luggage, unable to set it down. Missed ball games, parties, graduations, and cookouts—you fill in the rest of the blanks. Most everyone has something like this they can relate to.

So, I'm going to ask you a question: Are you getting the idea yet that communication plays a bigger role in your life than you ever imagined? It's the rock-solid foundation we spoke of earlier—the key to the entire life we lead—and without it, we are cursed with failure. I encourage you to dive deep into this valuable asset and take the time to learn how to improve your own ability to converse with anybody on any subject, even if you have little knowledge of the topic. You don't have to be an expert on a subject to hold a conversation with someone. Simply asking questions and then truly listening for the answer will provide you with key points. You'll also obtain enough valuable knowledge to stay engaged and on topic, and to show your ability and sincere interest in the conversation. This alone speaks volumes, and the people you're speaking with will pick up on it as well. People with polished communication skills can spot a player pretty quick, and they will realize when they're in a conversation with

Communication

someone who's looking for something self-serving, or who really has no interest in them at all, except for what they can do for him or her.

This learning curve does take time, but now that you know about it, you can no longer avoid it, and something must be done. There will be a blog or a Q &A section on my webpage, **Whoareyouandwhy.net,** where my readers can go and ask questions, and communicate with myself and others. I'll also have a list of recommended books that I feel have the most value to help increase your ability to communicate on many different levels. In the meantime, get out there and start speaking with new people. Make yourself strike up new conversations at coffee shops, or standing in line at your grocery store, the tire shop, or nail salon. Interesting people are all around you every day. You just haven't spent any quality time looking, speaking, and truly listening to what they have to say. You just never know; you may meet a future business partner, girlfriend, or maybe the person you needed to run into that has the answer to questions you have had for years. That's the beauty of new communication skills and conversations. They can take you to places you could only dream about before, and they can change your life's path instantly. So, get out there and make new contacts and friends. Your life will never be the same. There's no need to rush to the following pages. Practice your new skills, in the mirror and with close friends, to get started. I'll see you in Chapter 10, when you're ready.

Who are You, and Why?

Note: I didn't go into great detail about how to read body language or how to make things like NLP (Neuro-Linguistic Programming) work for you. You can study subjects like this on your own. What's more important at this stage is to learn how to ask useful questions and to listen wholeheartedly to the answers you receive. These two things can revolutionize your life. They're the place to start.

Communication

Notes

Who are You, and Why?

Notes

10
Character

10

Well, here we are: the final stepping stone on this journey. I find myself sitting here, in my office, wondering if I have made an impact on your life. Have I enlightened you regarding your true potential? And I trust that now you've identified many of the lies and conditioning that have been the shackles that have stopped you from being your true self—what we've all been told throughout our lives that has squashed or decreased our abilities to get ahead. Then there's the restrictions we placed upon ourselves due to the so-called knowledge experts that had no clue on how to raise us to be successful (because they didn't really know, only thought they knew). In all fairness, they taught us the same thing that was handed down to them. The knowledge I've been sharing with you was the key to my own success and is the reason I felt compelled to share it with as many as I could. Now I want to make this clear: In the last nine chapters, I was only pointing out what had been pointed out to me. I didn't come up with this knowledge. It was shared with me by people who had what I wanted, and who were willing to divulge it to me. Within the low percentage rate of successful people, there are many other qualities that have helped them become successful, but I think by far the most common is that they all have *great character*. This information is what separates the successful from the unsuccessful. You must first and

Who are You, and Why?

foremost know yourself and be happy with YOU. Without that, you'll stay on the rollercoaster ride. Being satisfied in your own body and mind allows you to move on to bigger and better things.

The first of these is being honest and having character. It's the starting point from which without you'll never build solid relationships with others. People will only follow you if they know without a doubt you can be trusted and that your word is golden. This is an unwritten rule that so few ever learn but that ranks up there with oxygen in importance. When people understand you'll always go above and beyond to do the right thing, even if it's not the best thing for you personally, and may cost you in the long run, they will flock to your door. That's true character, and no amount of money should ever have you lower your own personal demands for it, no matter what.

Character (noun) is described in the dictionary as the qualities that make a person or place distinct from everything else. Having admirable traits, such as honesty, responsibility, punctuality, morals, and ethics (You know, the very things we look for in others.), is like trying to find a flea in a hayfield these days. This must be a two-way street as well. You can't go looking for these traits in other people if you yourself don't carry them. People have lost track of what it means to be a great person.

It has been said that you can tell a lot about someone by simply reflecting on how they treat a person who can do absolutely nothing for them. Every person on this planet is dealing with some sort of issue daily and weekly. Let's say you meet someone

Character

when they are having a terrible day, and things just didn't go so well. You can tell something is bothering them, and instead of asking how they are doing, you label them too quickly as being rude, self-centered, maybe an egotistical ass, and never speak with them again. Most everyone has a few bad days a month, and you just happen to meet them on one of theirs, prejudge them, then find out later on down the road that his or her mother was very sick, in another city far away, and they couldn't be there to help out. You also find out this person has some of the same hobbies you have, and is very gifted, and is known to help anyone out that's willing to ask.

Now, let's handle that last example a little differently: You see this person is having a bad day, and you ask them, "How are you doing?" The conversation continues, and you find out about this other person in another town, and what they are dealing with that needs handled. You also come to find out you know someone in that same town that may be able to help. After digging a little deeper, the issue turns out to be that they needed some medication picked up that was prescribed, but they are too sick to go get it. You make a few calls, and your contact is able and willing to help out, and the problem is solved. Now, with the issue handled, the conversation continues on a much higher affinity level, to where the hobbies and other like-interests are the new topic. Boom, you just made two people happy with one simple heart-felt communication. It also turns out that your new acquaintance is willing to train you on a project you have been stuck on. Magical stuff? No, just a simple act of kindness from a person with true character.

Who are You, and Why?

You know, maybe if we took the time to focus on the other guy a little more, we would have fewer bad days as well. I've been dealing with a bad day and have run into someone who was dealing with an even worse day. I stopped and chatted with them a bit, with true interest, and then, all of a sudden, my day wasn't so bad. I also helped them have a better day.

Character and your word are EVERYTHING. Without it, you are nothing. There are many great people still out there, with good hearts, who are looking for others with the same characteristics. Though not so easy to find, they are the golden goose eggs we need to look for daily. When multiple people with this kind of integrity, ethics, and character gather as one, anything can be accomplished. All being on the same page, sharing a common goal, and everyone looking out for each other can help pull all the stops on a project once stuck in a ditch.

To have a high level of character, you must first have it within yourself to say what you do and do what you say. Lying to yourself and not being accountable for your lack of action on plans you lay out for yourself isn't what you should be after. Character is the glue that keeps everything together when things look gloomy. I was in the middle of my first *almost* filing bankruptcy (there were 3 different ones), but my word and character got me through all that mess. I had promised clients product delivery dates and didn't have the money to do it, so instead of breaking my word, I borrowed some money from my father to finish what I promised. I had to put myself in even more debt to keep my word. If I hadn't done this at that point in time, my character would have been scarred in the business world (that kind of word travels very fast), and would have led to the end of me. Character can never be sacrificed for any amount of money. A missed deadline can set you back a bit if it occurs occasionally, but taking measures to decrease that from happening over and over is building better character, and people respect that. Anyone in business has had to deal with angry customers for many different reasons, but it's how you rectify the issue that helps them with the decision to either continue with you or tell you to go pound salt. This kind of character must be maintained in every aspect of your life—keeping a dinner date, or showing up to a school play; being on time for a scheduled meeting—pretty much following through with all promises you make to everyone. Yes, this can be tough at times when there are circumstances beyond our control, but planning ahead will keep many of those issues at bay: leaving a little earlier, cutting an unnecessary conversation short to make a meeting on time, getting out of bed on time, and also looking ahead for things that may affect a timeline, and confronting them.

Relationships of all kinds revolve around character: from your wife or girlfriend to husbands and boyfriends, coworkers, business partners, a store clerk, the environment, and those in need. This kind of living must be a staple in your daily living, and it sets an example for others as well. Most people strive to do good, but dropping character requirements on themselves knocks them out of balance with their surroundings; and trust me, people see the bad long before they see the good. I've met many people over the years, who were so far out in left field with their character

Who are You, and Why?

that nobody would trust them: self-serving pricks that only worried about "What's in it for me?" and never, "What can I do for you?" They can't ever be trusted, and you should stay clear of them. Once you're labeled as someone with *no or bad character*, it's next to impossible to wash that label off. You can burn lots of bridges living like that, but people still do it daily and wonder why they can't make it in this world. Flawless character will take you farther in this world than money or anything else.

Take some time right now and do a little soul searching. Look back at some issues where you didn't keep your end of the bargain, or when character was sacrificed to better suit you than the issue at hand. Write them down, as there will be more than a few. Then go back to the ones you can fix, and fix them. Make up for the missed date, football game, or school play, or paying off an unpaid loan—anything you didn't follow through with and make it right. People will notice the effort, and you can start to gain back some of the trust that was lost. Continue on this journey until you've cleaned up every last one of your messes, no matter how long it takes.

Clearing a conscience relieves a lot of the baggage that keeps you down. When we clean our messes up, it gives us a sense of satisfaction (or a cleansing). And when we violate character law, it sticks with us, as we know we didn't keep our word or promise. That stuff piles up like rocks. We carry it around like a curse, hindering our progress because we're more focused on the wrongs we committed. And in the end, we lose focus of the issues at hand.

Character

You really must clean up the past to prepare you for the future. You need to put some sort of metering device upon yourself to keep those out-of-character moments from coming back and happening all over again. Will there be more moments of relapse? You bet your ass there will be, but when you take notice—and you will now—you can turn it around immediately instead of it festering into a shit storm. The best way I know how to do this is by redefining what the past and even the present means. Let's say you missed a delivery to one of your clients last week, and you know he's going to be pissed. There's a couple of things you can do. First, redefine what you're feeling. You don't have to feel guilt over missing the delivery. You can just as easily say to yourself, *"Yes, I missed a delivery, but I'm going to make it right today. This means I can feel good about myself."* You can also wipe away any discomfort you may be having about meeting with your client: *"I've been consistent with and loyal to this customer for a long time. Our relationship will survive this, because I'm going to make things right today."* And finally, you can define what you're going to do today to make things right: *"I'm going to give my customer a 30% discount on his purchase today, which will be enough to cover his losses from last week. I'm certain he will be satisfied with this. He won't be happy about the missed delivery, but there's nothing I can do about that. I can only move forward with integrity."*

I want you to understand that development of good character, self-improvement, and personal development is a daily challenge that isn't easy but is a must—if you really want to live a happy, fulfilling life. We want our lives filled with great people, nice houses and cars, and all the things that make you happy along

Who are You, and Why?

the way. Best of all is the creation of the mindset that comes with knowing you do as much good as you can, each and every day, before placing your head on that pillow at night.

Well, here we are at the end of the journey. I feel a sense of relief from actually creating the best book I think possible at this time. I have so much more to share, and just may do that at a later date, but I am confident you've received some of the best information to make your stand. I want you to live every day to the fullest, no matter what cards you're dealt. Keep your head up at all times, stay focused, and never let anyone—including yourself—tell you something can't be done.

PS.

I want to thank you again for picking up this book and reading it to the end. You can't give it away. You need to place it on your bookshelf to read again at a later date. I guarantee you didn't get 100% of the value in the pages. That usually takes a multitude of reads over time. It has been said that it takes about 40 plus reads of a single book to get an 80% knowledge of its content. I would ask you, if this book did change your life, to recommend it to as many people as you think could benefit from its content. Get out there and start living YOUR life, not the one chosen for you.

Character

Notes

Who are You, and Why?

Notes

TESTIMONIALS

What an illustrious honor! Brian, I struggle to place a value on the discussions and knowledge that you have shared with me. My walk towards greatness now takes a straighter path as a result of your impartations.

—Eddie L. Blacknell
President/CEO of JUMPOUT INTERNATIONAL

I've only known Mr. Brian Penso (aka Uncle Larry) for a few years. In that time, I've enjoyed Brian's entertaining way of sharing his knowledge, experience and communication skills. No sugar coating here just clear and simple communication tips that will work for your fishing buddy or your business partner! This is one of the few books I will read over and over again.

—Karen White
Former VP JPMorgan Chase; CEO & President of KBW Consulting Houston, TX

I have known Brian for over 8 years. I was impressed with him the first day we met. I could tell this guy "got it" and saw things differently. Over the years we became business associates and good friends. The more time we spent with each other, the more I realized he brought a very powerful and unique perspective to the situation. I worked for 20+ years at the highest levels of two Fortune 300 companies. In addition, I own several companies as well. I recently retired from Corporate America at the age of 42 and I can honestly say that

Who are You, and Why?

Brian had an impact and played a part in my relatively early exit from that arena. There have been many instances in negotiating, and reviewing new opportunities that I have thought, "What would Brian do in this situation?" It's amazing how powerful a change in your mindset can be and it can come from one idea. Brian has brought a ton of those ideas to the masses with this book. I'm so glad he decided to sit down and take the time to pass on those thoughts to a lot of people that weren't as lucky to have met Brian like I was.

—Casey Salge
Multiple Business Owner

The knowledge and experience that Brian shares is truly the core of what is required to create success and get whatever it is that you want from life. I would not have broke away from the corporate world to pursue creating my own success in life through multiple business ventures, had it not been for the principles that Brian teaches and lives by.

—Jacob Wernitznig
Realtor and Professional Network Marketer
Houston, TX

Business in front Party in the Back! Uncle Larry aka Brian Penso. He has been an inspiration and a true leader in all aspects of my life. Brian will never candy coat anything and tell you nothing but the straight honest truth. It has been great to have him as a friend and mentor in my life. Looking forward to what is to come as we continue down the journey of life.

—David Jones

ABOUT THE AUTHOR

Brian Penso was born in Barberton, Ohio, on February 23, 1966 to Andy and Joanne Penso. He spent his first decade being a normal trouble maker (to say the least). His father purchased an existing concrete business in 1977 and moved to the country in southern Ohio. It was in this environment that Brian was raised to work hard and help whomever was in need, no matter when or where that need arose. It was a way of life.

Brian started his first company at the age of 15, building fishing lures and selling them to local fisherman and marines, following the footsteps of his self-employed father. Well, as many young people do, he took some bad turns along the way and found more trouble than he was looking for. So, at the age of 21 he packed up his belongings and with $250 in his pocket moved to Houston, Texas.

He began as a journeyman meat cutter for a large store but found that working for someone wasn't his cup of tea. He decided the solution was to start another company in the concrete industry, which he knew well from growing up at his father's factory. Unfortunately for Brian, people considered him still wet behind the ears and were not so ready to do business with him, even though he claimed to be the best in the business. The problem was he didn't have the track record they needed to trust him.

Who are You, and Why?

Thus the long journey started. There were many failures, and Brian lost everything multiple times (not having enough money to feed himself on a daily basis and living in old dirty warehouses with no heat or hot water for many years). The money he did have went to food and tennis balls for his trustworthy sidekick, Abby, a dog he had rescued along the way. He claims "That crazy pup got me through the worst times of life, and she never gave up on me."

At one point, after a company didn't pay for some products, Brian was down to his last few dollars. He was at the end again. He sold everything he had to pay off the debts he had created and was looking to move back home, defeated—just as many figured he would. However, before he could do anything else, a light came on, and he decided to give it one more go. That dedication, grit and a pure desire to not fail took him on another 15-year journey that paid off with dividends; Brian created one of the largest companies in his industry, with clients spanning from coast to coast. He has also accumulated a vast knowledge on failing but not giving in, which is what makes the pages in this book so priceless. The journey you're about to take is the blueprint he uses daily. Note: Brian continued on to build several more companies that are still up and running today. Enjoy your journey

Made in the USA
Coppell, TX
09 August 2023